The Tainted Files: Evolution of Poetic Style

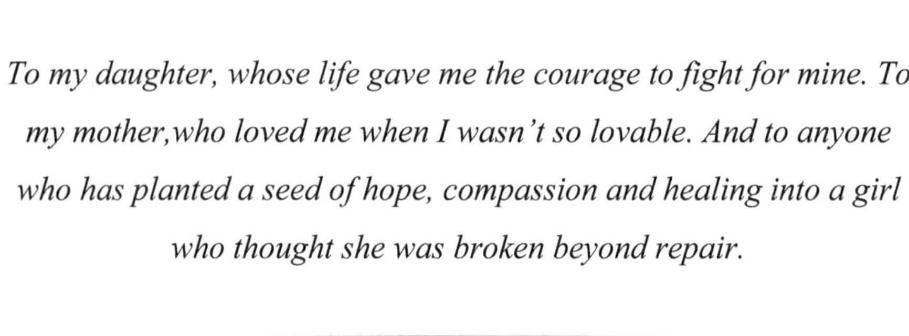

To my daughter, whose life gave me the courage to fight for mine. To my mother,who loved me when I wasn't so lovable. And to anyone who has planted a seed of hope, compassion and healing into a girl who thought she was broken beyond repair.

CONTENTS

Acknowledgements/ Gratitude(s)

I want to give an eternal thank you to all those who I don't have the capacity in this setting to pay honor and homage to. I cannot thank every person name by name who has inspired me, lent kind words and encouragement. Some of these individuals even let me sleep on their couches over the years. I almost didn't have the courage to put this collective together and then remembered all of you who told me I had a story to share and that like you all have helped me, that I could help someone out there.

My Creator,

Thank you for life itself and the borrowed time you have mercifully bestowed upon a wretch like me. Thank you for placing a lyric in my heart that helped me move in times of seeming futility. For your unfailing love, direction, provision, and protection. You have placed angels on my path and always led me back to the light of your infinite comfort.

Mommy,

My beautiful and enduring mother. For all you have been, done, sacrificed, and let slide. I hope one day to make you proud and that you see that none of the trials were in vain, no matter the outcome. You have shown up and suited up my whole life and I thank you. I love you. Thank you for walking with me. Especially when it was hard.

My Munchkin,

I love you beyond all the stars in the sky. You are my inspiration and my hope. When you get older, I pray you understand and take a different path and can use my experiences to deter you from a dark one. I am blessed by your existence, and you are a beautiful expression of God and His love. Always stay true to yourself and Love.

Ray Ray,

My road dawg, my sister, my best friend. I want to thank you for being a solid friend and sister and for being a real- life day to day example of change, growth, responsibility, and recovery. I look up to you and always will and thank you for never looking down on me as you reached your hand out to help me get back on my feet. For reminding me you can always add to your "family" and what "home" means.

Thank you. Always.

Stephan,

For helping me muster up the courage to put this collective together, for many years of conversation that led to a true bond and for being a mentor and friend. I truly appreciate your presence on my journey, thank you for being a part of it.

Poppy,

I thank you for being the Dad I never would have had without your willingness to step up, step in and stay. I love you and honor your permanent place in my heart and my life.

To all my family near and far that have known me my whole life and loved me anyway (you know who you are). I truly am grateful for the times we shared on this path and even through distance and time the memories we shared are imprinted in my heart and mind and I will forever love you all.

To the men I've loved and lost,

For planting a seed of romance and harsh lesson of the impending need for self-love and self-respect, thank you. For what we shared in moments of intimacy individually will always be held sacred.

Grandma,

My angel once on earth and now in heaven, you held our family together and still do. We are always connected in spirit, and I will always miss you and remember that the strength in your blood still runs through my veins. I love you. Rest in Peace my lady.

Dr. Brenda Combs (C.E.O./BRC Publishing):

Thank you for taking my hand through this process to put this all together. For the many talks we have had and the gems of wisdom you have dropped on me are priceless. You are an example of transformation and the possibilities out there despite circumstance. I am forever grateful to work with you and look forward to more collaborations!

To the countless wise, strong, tolerant members of all the anonymous groups:

Thank you for the seeds of love, hope, recovery, change, unity and community I so desperately needed that gave me a place where I finally belonged and felt more understood than I ever have. I'm learning how to live because of you. We don't shoot our wounded" and for that I am thankful. When I crawled back time after time, there were many who scoffed at me, and the rest of you told me to "keep coming back."

For those who didn't kick me as I was down and even for those who did from the bottom of my heart thank you.

To the friends I've met, bonded with, left behind and lost along the way (anywhere everywhere I've ever traveled):

We may or may never cross paths again, you may never read this, but your energy lives in my heart and our experiences helped shape me for the better. Thank you.

Introduction

Welcome to the pages of my mixtape. I hope and pray that in my words someone reading this can relate. When I was younger, I dreamed of being someone special, I've come to learn I am no one special but I am somebody. I was full of life and zest, I was unafraid. Things changed as it always does. The way I experienced the world and the way I felt it looked at me. I never thought to express myself, I never knew how nor felt confident or safe. I was expressive in all the wrong ways. Through the years I picked up a pen and found it was at times my only friend. If it were not for others in my life encouraging me to express myself and to put this project together, I would still have these poems tucked away in various notebooks thinking no one would want to hear them.

Many may never know how they have contributed to my life and in this book; my wish is too shed light on emotions you may have felt, or issues you have experienced or even couldn't fathom. My name is Indya Renee. This is my story. If you happen to vibe with it, I give God all the glory. I am grateful for the blessings come after harsh lessons and I am blessed to have seen one more day; that's opportunity and grace. I share with you my heart in these pages. I am a recovering addict. I am also someone who is diagnosed with mental illness, trauma and has not been successful at long term recovery in different areas. I do however write my struggles and experience, my vulnerabilities, my lyrics; because in all the ups and downs we all have some common emotions and things we all deal with.

I am no one special but striving to be a better person every day and have a new way of experiencing life. I have fallen and been graced by a power greater than myself as well as much help from others that held my hand to help me to get back up. I have been encouraged to share my words and I hope and pray that they can touch someone as I have been touched and helped along the way. I want to thank you for taking the time on your individual journey to spend time with me on mine. Please don't forget that we all have a song in our heart only we can sing. Our purpose is to sing to someone we may not know that needs to hear it in the way only you can. Sing your song...and please remember mine.

Volume I: Matters of the Heart

(Side A)

"The Lust of Passion"

Words

It's morning, a beautiful morning to say the least.

The past few weeks I've missed the morning; the sun, the chirping of birds and the grace of rising in inspiration and ambition that waking up before noon brings.

Sometimes, I look at sleep as a great way to not only recharge but escape from the realities, responsibilities, and stressors of the physical world.

Unfortunately, that cuts me off from promising opportunities and the joy of grace to have a new day to live life and seize it like the gift it is.

However, there are times when the activity in my slumber is no more pleasant than my perceived strife. I am and always have been blessed. We all, are. When my perspective shifts to gratitude the world isn't so scary, and I lack nothing. I must remind myself in the darkest hours that I am not alone. I am not a lost cause. The creator has a purpose for each one of us and I am included in that.

This is howI do it~

I know how to do it; How to make his toes curl

I know how to put a smile on his face; how to "be a good girl"

I can keep a secret, I will never tell

When they ask about him I'll always say "doesn't ring a bell"

My lips ignite a fire that burns within

He's reminded of his softer side when guiding his hand on my skin

Lust so strong is considered a sin

Feelings so real they bear no end

I know how to do it; how to let him be a man

I know how to let him take all that he can

I am a beautiful woman deep in his penetration

I know how to demonstrate my appreciation

He keeps me guessing; I keep him satisfied

He thrives on the passion I eagerly provide

I am the aid that helps him sleep at night

Wrong in many ways but in many ways so right

When he's not on my mind he's present in my sight

I know how to do it; I know how to please

I know how to make him drop to his knees

He never has to beg or plead

I give myself willingly

With him I am alive and free

He tastes of joy and ecstasy

I want to give him all of me

I know how to do it; how to satisfy

The secret lies between my thighs, inside my kiss, around my hips

And at the stroke of my fingertips.

Just my Imagination

Consumed bound in fantasy electricity surges

Igniting every dormant trace of the sun's imprint on my flesh

Pain is irrelevant, nor does time exist

Infatuation is the catalyst of our long-awaited kiss

It's in his embrace I am free tentatively from my cage

Intertwined savagely fueled lust

Ignited in obsession touching souls

Together transparent, vulnerably, authentic, yet so coy;

Unwavering affection

We are who we are

Love in the night always thriving in the stars

Rules don't apply; not tonight

Zeal motivates every expression of passion

Caught in the rapture and resting

We don't look back savoring every juicy moment of bliss

The taste creates an insatiable hunger to CONQUER

Edging closer to explosion, arousing ecstasy

Reality violently rushes in taking over

He is gone

I prance my feet disappointingly and return to my cage.

Longing

I haven't felt this way in a while

The way he makes me feel just makes my panties want to drop

I'm just waiting for this romance to flop

Wondering if this crush will go the long mile

Damn, he's got me a little open

My body melts the way he strokes it

I can be myself with him, he seems to adore me

I love the way he kisses me slowly…

His personality just makes me weak

His stature and swagger makes me drop to my knees

I wonder what he sees in me

My last encounter with a man was truly damaging

Is this all too good to be true

He makes me feel like I am beautiful

I really want this experience to last

He doesn't make me feel like just a piece of ass to grab

I just want someone that I can trust

I felt closer to him with every thrust

Honesty and connection

Well that's a must I desire more than empty lust

We will see where things evolve to

To him I’ll be kind, to myself I’ll stay true

We can do whatever we want to do

We’ll let it ride sit back and just cruise

Enchantment

Bound in the lure of this enchanting fantasy
So far away, yet so close in the same embrace
A forbidden romance that will never take place
Yet the skies open up when I look into his eyes
And his heart melts when his hands are on my thighs
Moments spent together causes time to fly
Insatiable hunger for each other boils deep inside
Flowers bloom
The sun brightly shines
Joy lights up the sky
In another lifetime
this could be just fine there'd be no crime of
crossing the line
Even the grandest canyon couldn't house
the feelings of ecstasy being aroused
No others would be allowed around
I'd never come down back to the ground
Floating higher with every sound
Of the forbidden passion I've dreamed about.

Magnetic Obsession

There was a magnetic orgasm between our eyes; instant obsession.

Preoccupied thoughts of manic idolatry

Shared between two fleshy beings

Caught in the rapture

Sheer excitement and zeal

We are love

We are love

Unconditionally

May I be his sweet coquette?

May I entice his lust?

If him not be mine than sadly

I am a lonely cheap courtesan waiting patiently for love

Lest I be the fatale to lead him away.

Promiscuity (XXX)

Juices from his cum taste to me like heaven

He has other girls I know, but when he's with me

I'm the only one

He thrives on my pounding passion

We thrash our bodies absent from the sun

I ride him until he smiles

He goes the extra mile

I stroke him up and down

His cock is mine to mount

He asks how many times I came knowing I actually lost count

I pause whatever I'm doing when he tells me to come around

He tells me to be quiet when he hits my G spot

The neighbors might say I'm too loud

When someone mentions his name in conversation

I never make a sound

My passion is the key to pandoras box

No man shall ever return once it's unlocked

When I slowly lick the shaft and

Drop my throat on his spot he moans with cheerful agony

And tells me not to stop

He fits just right and I am just so tight

I suck on his finger while he feels my insides

I nibble on his bottom lip while he smashes me from behind

There are no boundaries they faded over time

Yet I am not his and he is not mine

Still when we unite in lust and worship we are two of a kind

If it weren't for us devouring the night

The sun would have no reason to shine.

Twisted Reflections

I love it when you're inside me

I hate it when you deny me the affection my heart is desiring

In itemizing your flock I am dispensable

When you talk I am convincible

Upon finishing I am reprehensible

You tell me what to do and I am permissible

I've seen you somewhere else in this life

I think I may have confused you as Mr. Right

You always show up in the poems I write

We only make love in the absence of light

I won't tolerate being played and abused

I won't sacrifice my pride just to be in love with you.

Co-Dependent Delusions of Addiction

Fighting this addiction trying to make better decisions

Seems as though my mind has always been afflicted

I write out and bare my soul memorize it then I spit it

I cry out and bare my soul pray out to God and then it's written

I never wanted my baby girl to feel alone

Though when it came to being a parent it seems

The streets I chose to roam

Every place I'd lay my head has never been my home

They told me to keep coming back but when I did

Everyone had moved on

I never traveled in a pack

I almost never had a crew

But when you came into my life

I opened up my soul to you

You show me a friendship and a bond

I forgot I ever knew

You were vulnerable with me

I was vulnerable with you

I'm beating a dead horse and it's turning over in his grave

I know we have to go

I know we have to go our separate ways

I hope and pray it just a matter of time

That we get to see each other again,

Hopefully at that time we will be in a healthier better place

I appreciate the way you made me embrace some self-respect

And when it came to your protection of me

I could never 2nd guess

We spent our lives for a while hip to hip and I want you to know

I have not one single regret

The only thing I wish was different is that

I would have been a better friend

I wish it never even started cause I never saw the end

Thank you for showing me I could love someone this way

Nothing to do at this point

With your looks or your handsome smile or face

I want us to be sober healthy happy and I want us to be safe

But at this time it seems together in our lives we do not have a place

Promise never to get forget about me

I'll be here for you in good and bad times

Just promise, promise, promise me

You will not try to take your own life

Promise me that you'll fight back from all the

Strife and fold all the cards you been dealt

Promise me that you'll seek HEAVEN now

Break the ties that have kept you in HELL

That one day I'll have my friend back

That knows me oh so well

That loved me despite me that gave a girl like me a story to tell

I don't know if you realize the impact you had in my world

I know you think you did me wrong but I can tell you I beg to differ

Sometimes I play the victim and

Our perspectives were always different

I like to talk a lot and yet you never fail to listen

Thank you for the time we spent

For not throwing me to the wolves

I did wonder at times if you were really down for me

If I was being used

Doesn't matter at this point

We both know the truth

I was down for you and you were down for me too

Really it just hurts just hurts I'm about to lose

The only real friend I've had in a while

And that person that person was you

Even if it was all a lie

Even if my feelings are a bit delusional.

Overdue Elegy~ (for theone that got away)

Excuse me,

If this seems a bit bold

I just want to share with you some things on my mind

I just got to let you know

From the first day I saw you

Til the last time we spoke

I experience a rare tingle in a private place

You and I have shared long ago

In a perfect world

You and I would run the night

When life got a little heavy you would stroke me back to life

The royalty in your melanin has blessed me

Yet not as often as I would like

Looking back when our eyes connected

I was caught a bit by surprise

Struggled to receive your admiration

My life path at the time was on a decline

And in reality our paths may never realign

However, the passion in our kiss however

Has lingered in my hopes over time

Recognition of the spirit within us

Soul meeting flesh caring of no one's opinion

Dominion and submission

No roles to play just positions

We call each other now and then

Check in to see "how things have been"

To me you will always be the friend I'll fondly adore

Until my time on earth ends

In my mind you a are majestic mahogany

Recipe for pleasure, zeal and orgasm in the night

I've touched myself miles away in memory of when our

Flesh and souls blended together

Lips of bliss like heaven

An intelligence that can't be understood or compared

During the saddest times in my life

You showed me you cared

I never made love to a King

Until the day you graciously penetrated and imprinted on me

I climbed your mountain

Ate the fruit off your tree

Touched my lips on the skin between your legs

And devoured you as a feast

I hope you'll remember me.

Remember me not as who the world may think of me

Remember me as the beautiful innocent young girl

You saw initially

Remember me please, don't ever forget

Please don't ever regret

The time we shared the way our souls connect

Somewhere in the future if our lives allow

I'd submit unto you

Make you proud

Scream and shout I would not let you down

Jump head first into your ocean

Your highest peak I would mount

Write sultry lyrics with you in bed and rejoice in your satisfied sound

There was no denying

When he entered inside me

Our souls touched and raged yet so quietly

Things got a little hectic so he passed right by me

From the corner of my lids

I spy him eyeing me

He knows the real truth with every thrust inside of me

Are we sinners for loving so blindly

Or are we pretenders who's love isn’t worth trying.

Exxxx

I can't change my past though

My spirit aches to just put it all behind me

I gently place it back on the shelf

His lack of trust in me constantly reminds me

He says I'm not the same girl he wanted

I say he only saw darkness when there was always a silver lining

Love or lust

Haves and have nots

Are we two souls who's lips never shall have locked?

I placed the key under his V-neck

He placed his lips on my forbidden fruit

I begged him not to stop

I am no longer a crumb on his lunch plate

Riding way too fast

Chased only to replace

We find our solace in resentment and fear

The bitter end of heartache

But is there a lining, silver in its color

Is there another out there like him?

Doubt it

I have never met another

I'm no longer interested in Tom, Dick, or Harry

Won't settle for yet another empty fantasy

I've been a deviant all my life

Still one day I hope for marriage

I refuse to graze on the grass of failed romance past

No longer selling myself short

Wrapping up my soul in every squeeze of my ass

Not wasting anymore time

When all signs lead to an over pass

I'm a queen in the making it's not up for debating

I've loved, I've lost

But I've been a little lonely lately

He was and is my dream

Sometimes our dreams die hard

I think about him all the time

His deepest love

I fantasized to uncover

He’s a man.

A real one

Maybe I'm too "hard core"

Do we leave it here at goodbye?

Or pick it up where we left off?

What is the Cost of Love?

Never had much money, but nothing in life is free

There are those things however, that inspire and motivate me

Driving me forward to my deepest hopes and wildest dreams

I've loved and I've lost

Paid more than what I was offered Love is the antidote and recipe

Heartbreak taught me to set it free if it isn't meant for me

The price of romance can sometimes be weighed out

In pounds of insecurities, unrequited efforts

Unrealized reciprocity

That's not the kind of love I seek Not the kind of love I need

Rejection is merely God redirecting me

The cost of love is a hefty price I sold for drugs

Chased to erase the pain almost followed them into my grave

Yearning for something to feel the void inside of me

The cost of love is how much you are willing to give up

In that regard I never felt I could off much

Not much to give

Was unsure of how to cherish and receive it

I pushed away so much love and still learning what it is

What is the cost of love?

What it is?

What it was?...

Is it the adorning touch, and quality time someone sets aside for you?

Love ;it has been light on my darkest night

Love has been the reason I cry at night

My motivation to try

Love saved my life multiple times

I may not be able to afford the price love costs but

I am willing to spend my last dime to share it with someone.

Somethin Somethin

It's nice to be called "pretty" and have someone in my life that can
Laugh and joke with me

The paradigms are shifting

Is this all more than a feeling?

Why do I think about you?

I would love you down

If I could be allowed to; my guard falls whenever I'm around you

I'm defenseless, apprehensive since we met

You snatched up all my resistance

And like a wrecking ball you plowed right through it

Anyone can thrash their bodies flesh to flesh

You inspire my creativity

I love the way our minds connect

It's pretty dope when I think about it

I wasn't looking for anything, had no idea what I wanted

But in this entanglement of sorts I think I found it

Divine timing with you I feel in alignment

But wait? Is this it?

I've never been good with intimacy or relationships

I just can't help to think about those lips

Not gonna lie all this is constantly on my mind

Maybe I am out of line

Or my imagination running away with me.

Finesse

"Turn around

Let me see how you fit in that dress, nah I don't want nothing else

Just want to make sure you look your best

Maneuvering through life with skill, minimal effort no regrets

Making sure I reap all the benefits

Discarding whatever doesn't fit

Leaving behind whatever's left

"Yeahhh…Mmmm"

"I'm digging the vision and I like how it's coming to fruition

Love it when my needs and wants get met,

When what I want comes easily

But I'm always ready to put the work in"

I want my cake

I want to eat it too

I like team players and little resistance to the rules

No sweat

Full Breast

Good Sex

Nothing compares to some commas on a thick check

Look at me

Make it clap

No going back you cool with that?

If you need a little inspiration

I got a cure for that

Say less

Silver tongue finesse on my breath

Pillow chat; no naps

No sleep, nobody got time for that

Casino bets private sex

Life is a gamble, take the risk

See what happens next.

~(1:11)~

It's 1:11am

And as the weekend begins

I sit here struggling not to think about you

About us all

The trajectory of our lives and what we have been through

The number that sparked a connection

How we began, beginning to end

All you meant to me over the years

Honestly some days you were my only friend

My confidant, My lover, My protector ,My mentor

Somebody who seemed to actually care

The passion, exchange and joy I felt when I fell for you

I wonder if you still feel the same way too

Has too much damage been done?

Can we shift our perspective?

Transmute our view?

Mistakes were made between us two

Heavy is the guilt we carry

The shame of disappointment every time I connect eyes with you

Our hearts once beat to the same rhythm

Lately it's push and pull, conquer and subdue

The disdain you feel for me is so real to you

Hurt people, hurt people but I never meant to hurt you

We are human, doing the best we can do

I saw into your soul

You saw into mine too

Your adorning gaze made me feel so beautiful

I appreciate you, I pray that you know

Can we go back to where things were before...?

When you tilted my crown

When you were comfortable with me being me and

I admired the man that I saw

The time we spent together means a lot to me and

I miss you when you aren't around

When our time was focused on the grind

All issues and drama were left behind

An ambitious place I had dreamed of yet could never find

The most innocent thought of you makes my whole body tremble

So much damage ensued

Now I appear to be someone you don't resemble

Is this the place where we finally let go

Distant memories resentful shadows?

Never loved no one like you before

As you were trying to lace my boots I stood still and lost control

I just hope you know

You became my family when I had none

You earned my submission

Your dominance fed me to satisfaction

I understand that we have to journey on

What we started is what my heart wants

You shared with me pieces of you that

I'll cherish from this moment on.

Intrigue

Love can be blinding but so very exciting

Takes you on a journey too self-reflection baring all your deepest

wounds to the surface breaking barriers and walls

Love can be so inspiring there is no way of hiding

So overwhelming, so inviting

Things like your heart break and fall apart

As you yearn eagerly to keep it all together and keep on trying

Love brings the best out of me

Joy and pain balance each other out like ashes to the flame

Life takes its twists and turns, you lean forward

Stumble over the lessons, appreciate the blessings and you learn

Love is complete in itself, holds no grudge

Has no price to pay, no prize to earn

Lust doesn't last long

Honest motives lead the way to freedom in love

Whereas there was none

We are mirrors in one reflection

Pulled in so many directions

I am beautiful and safe intertwined inside loves affection

I am seen, heard and understood

but leap of faith love I must take

Dances in the ring with rejection and heartbreak

We show up to love anyway

And stare fear and struggle in the face.

Volume I: Matters of the Heart

(Side B)

"Heartbreak, Aches & Love"

Words

When I look back in hindsight at the things that once defeated and left me bewildered are placed into perspective with reason and I am blessed with clear sight and I will admit it can be brutal. To see all the ways, I have fallen short of utter and fatal failure is a bittersweet sense of gratitude laced with shame; that I still have a chance to change it but the reality of the failure.

I can see the ways I allowed myself to be chewed up, used up and spit out by the closest ones in my circle. My most embarrassing secrets and insecurities exposed in vulnerability and humiliation. The gossip, betrayal and bullying that made me who I am today.

I review the nights I left my daughter yearning for parents that were absent and trapped in the vicious cycle irresponsibility and addiction. I wonder at times my true identity, who am I really? The woman I could be from within or the woman I have been on the outside. Most of my life has been trying to get "there"; anywhere but "here" grasping to escape the torment of what I felt inside that can only be summed up in self-centered hopelessness.

Since I was young, I dreamed of being anyone but myself and had no idea who that really was. Still figuring that out. I tried a life on social media to fill a pretentious void and came up short never measuring up to everyone I beheld in comparison. I am guilty of the old saying "judging my insides by someone's outsides" and it always left me lacking.

There are many people on my journey who loved me through the darkest and ugliest times in my life. They straightened my crown. My mother and aunt reminded me of the blood running through my veins and the city that helped to mold me. I had many friends who saw the best in me when I presented my worst angles. I could never repay every single person who lifted me up as I tore myself down.

I decided in my heart to not give up, no matter how bad I want to sometimes or how rational it seemed at other times. I have hope today because of my higher power's spirit and the angels placed in my path. I choose to never forget the embarrassing/humiliating, tragic, shameful, painful, or hateful spectacles I have encountered on my journey. I will never forget them and hopefully in my writing you will have a clearer picture of what I mean. We cannot appreciate the sunshine without the rainstorm.

A Kind of Love

Love.

I want love Not any love

Not just because

Not the kind of love that makes your pussy cream

The kind of love that makes your spirit free

Love.

I want a love that believes in me

Hopes and dreams

I want the forever memories

I don't want the kind of love that flees

The kind of love that sneaks and cheats

I want the love that encompasses everything

All my needs 50/50

Never shifting but growing and uplifting

Booty calls and FWBs

No longer have a place in between my knees

They say in your lifetime you will meet three

May my ride or die love that was taken from me

Rest handsomely in peace

My cup over flows with the love from my homies

The love from my baby girl and of course my phenomenal mother

I've grown in learning to love myself

I have accumulated self-appreciation

Since I was freed from hell

But I crave the kind of love that makes you just melt

When no one else matters just you and them

I accept rejection as a form of the universe's divine protection

I am learning to love my own reflection

Love.

The love that makes time fly by

Love that didn’t cause the tear in your eye

Love that loves your short hair or full weave

Love that may just get down on one knee

I'm done searching I'll be ready when he arrives

I want it now yes but

It’s Gods time not mine

Love that will be there in good and bad times

Love that encourages me to let my light shine

I don't know if this even exists

But having this kind of love is on my bucket list

I’m thinking Disneyland, Paris and coast to coast road trips

But it seems as though he doesn't exist.

Struggle to Agape

Struggling to love.

Looking back I had no real idea of what it really was

I "loved" things for a short time

A guy if he was fine; but to look into my eyes and see

a reflection of someone beautiful whole and divine

I would be lying

To say I didn't love sex meant I moved onto the next

If you had what I needed it was all I could offer at best

I could say I loved my child much more than a sentimental smile and

Made a life worthwhile with no regrets

I had still been lying to myself

I do not understand love

Could not recognize what truth and sacrifice in action it was

I was supposed to love myself and

I struggled to love and excelled in a seeming lost cause

That is my biggest hurdle and fall

How do I love what I hated the most

What makes sense for my life now at 30yrs old

How do I survive the hope for a life of joy, family and
be in relationship with the Divine when the light starts to shine
I am once again strangled to near death by my own mind
I pray and meditate for healing inside
I wonder if I am capable of love
Or am I merely a rotten seed of the unrighteous kind
Its hard but love has won battles for me
And it is still not something I comprehend
I am apparently years, learnings and deed behind
Only able to bleed my silent cries
With the ink seeping through my pen
Every mood swing
Every other night.

Someone(s) I used to know

I trusted you and betrayed myself

Showed you my wounds; you laughed as you threw salt in them

A kind of hurt I had never felt

I'm a survivor of your lies and belittlement

So hurt, void and angry

Brought out the worst in myself

I learned some things I will never forget

I am not perfect but I do not deserve this

Toxic friendships and unhealthy motives

Bruises and wounds compounded by my "closest friends"

Putting down my cross

Picking up my pen

I am guilty of whatever

I provoked in you that built your provoked resentment

Ill willed karmic vengeance

Absent of and love compassion

Lacking all forgiveness

Pretentious sentiment

I am worthy of love just because

Grateful and looking forward

For what lies behind me is already done

You are just someone(s) that I "used to know"

Forgiveness is key

My perspective is keen; choosing to live and love myself

Because that is exactly all that I need

Releasing your hold on me; closing the door on the painful memories

Inspired to change day by day with grace

Gazing in the mirror to see my reflection

The shattered pieces that didn't break

Gazing in the mirror I see love and grace

Accepting my flaws and fragilities

Loving myself taught me to see

I don't need friends who treat me like their enemy.

Divine Separation

It's best at this time, that we go our separate ways

First, I want to say please understand Please listen

Forgive me for being so codependent

I thought of you a friend in my life?

I begged you into it

Now its ruined because of grand expectations laced with resentment

I held out my arms; you closed your palm

I pursued a friendship in you but it was all based off

Whatever substance we were on

Now I'm left alone as you carry on

The people on your life say I'm just a crazy one

I will not be ashamed my heart will never change

I do not regret what we had

Just the time I will never get back

Say what you mean; Do what you say

I have no trust anymore

Heart black as led

I'm changing lanes; It was all in my head it was all just a game

So now I truly know my place

I know what to do; my efforts will change

I thought I had a friend my flame was doused in the rain

I wore my heart on my sleeve and learned to dance in the rain

To myself I'll be true; for your apparent good I'll stay away

You never should have to beg for someone to prove

The words they say, they must show you

In love and lies deception rules

So stuck on thinking I was in love with you

The reality is; the blind truth

We never were anything other than the drugs we used

I'll stay in the background from here on; you may wonder where I am

But I'll be long gone

I'm not running from anything

I'm flying towards the sun

My soul told me not to chase you

But as always, I didn't listen.

Desperate Emancipation

Dying for emancipation from this unintentional

misguided, unrequited infatuation

Dying inside for a little reciprocation

To no avail within his rejection of my affection lies my devastation

English words cannot describe the pain I hide inside

I smile and I giggle and lie awake crying at night

People ask me how I'm doing but under the mask I hide

I see my reflection instantly close my eyes; it's an ugly sight

Alone in a world full of people yet no one is by my side

Growing stronger every time I learn a lesson

Every heartache, every heartbreak became my greatest blessings

Any rejection I've faced was God's redirection

Looking back with no regrets just self-reflection

Laced-up my boots, gonna keep stepping

You lost a good one in me

If you see me in the street, look in the other direction.

Blue Lights

You tell me you remember those blue lights

However I remember every night

You know your memory lives in everything I write

Your presence impacted every aspect of my life

For a while we lived our lives side by side

I don't know if you care about it

I still cry sometimes every tear gets me high

I know you love me no matter what you show

Unfortunately to me you felt like more than the flame to my soul

Every one tells me to run far away but my heart says no

What am I to you; just a wooden stool; a broken tool?

Society says I'm just a fool

The jokes on me right for loving you

So sad by the situations I put us through

I just wanted to be there for you

I pray those blue lights shine through

I prayed one day my love would break through

Those blue lights in the starry night were so beautiful

Almost as beautiful as you

Stay true

Stay you

The rose-colored lens I saw you through

Are the reason my soul is blue

Realizing how they were so blinding

Lost myself in those lights I fell out of alignment.

Envy

Apparently everything isn’t as it appears

We've both fallen victim to lies that once seemed so sincere

Unsure and insecure about the way that we feel

Trapped in a hostile situation

Because we kept our lips sealed

And emotions arise when the truth is revealed

And the trust we once had lost all of its appeal

Do we throw our hands up the air

And act as if we never cared?

Green eyed monsters never like to share

But wasn't it just you and me

When no one else was there?

So to end things over a mistake

Just would not be fair

Neither of us can properly wear a halo

We both get hurt over the things we shouldn't know

Tensions rise and our reaction is to lose control

Screaming in the others face

And pushing them out the door

Deep inside to each other

We are the only ones that matter

We think about all the good times

The passion, the kisses and the laughter

Is it worth it to us to keep running after?

It all depends on how we end this chapter.

Collateral Damage

Seeing as how I'm just your "collateral damage"

I'll add my name to the list of those you have yet wreak havoc

You are now just another name in the book

Of my soulful passage

You should have never come into my life

If you only meant to cause static

The moment I saw your charming smile

I knew I should have seen straight through it

You would be the devil to bring me my demise

but bonding with you I never would have knew it

It's been only a short while

But my life crumbled at your pretty feet

You passed me by, you made me cry

Your touch though made me weak

The needle a has you bound

Your love lies in the cc's

I have realized at this point

You are incapable of loving you or anyone

Especially not me.

I saw hope for tomorrow in the hazel eyes

That glared back at me

Your perfect white smile was an essence

Of heaven to me

The talks we have when your sober

My soul couldn't help but to cling

It seems like for all the hearts I've broken

Karma is returning to me

I thought that we were close

Even soul mates you said one time

But in reality I am not yours and you are not mine

Everything we had was mostly built up on a lie.

Lost Smiles

It's the first time I've smiled in a minute

I knew my life would change in some way as

I begged him to be in it

In the beginning it seemed like we were winning

Then the progression of addiction

Reminded us that we really didn't

Another month has passed on and now I'm hooked

He embedded on my soul

Now the shackles that bind me can't be shook

Someone, God-Please help me save my life before its took

I need to write another chapter, rewrite the story,

Change the ending in my book

He had the most beautiful smile ever seen

I was unaware that the blood running through his veins

Would bring me to my knees

Now my future lies in the Ccs

My baby girl doesn't stance a chance against this affliction

Her parents are nowhere to be seen

It's been the 1st time I've smiled in a while

The other day I saw my daughter and embraced her

Like a mother should her child

It's just we both know I won't be around

Going through withdrawal and separation

Mommas got to figure something's out

Had a home, job, and a car

Now I'm surfing from the streets to the couch

Been lost for so long I don't know if I'll ever be found

It's been a while since I smiled and I mean it

The shit in my veins is worse than the chains

Containing me to have to break them and wean it

I’ve been a slave to this insanity

But the beauty and bliss I found in the trenches of tricks

I thought at one point was the escape I needed

God does for me what I can't do for myself

I been a lost little girl

my existence has dwelled in the pits of he

I may not have committed murder

But I've caused a lot of death

Haven't had many relationships

But I have had a lot of sex

My unmanageable presence causes nothing but distress

I feel like no one trusts me anymore

No one would care if I was dead

My smiles lately are not fake

And when I do smile my laughter bellows from my soul

When I am spending time with myfamily

I am grateful for this day

Trying my hardest to make a change

I believe in myself right now

I haven't smiled in a while.

Old Friend

I thought of you my friend for a time

My rose colored eyes truly believed you'd always be in my life

I turned to you for comfort

My aid to sleep at night

Things got real quickly and I saw your ugly side

Energies spun around

Tried to knock me down seeking to conquer and divide

Loving you brought me to embarrassment

Unbuckling my confidence and my pride

So insecure in my own skin

Wasn't living

One foot in the grave; I was dying

So afraid to leave you I could rarely sleep at night

Alone in the absence of light

All I could do was cry

Time would fly when I was with you

I thought I could trust our bond

Then you took away your consolation

Left me high alienated and dry

My fragile life, my hopes my aspirations

Precious memories passed me by

Loving you became the catalyst

for every tear I shed in both eyes

I adored you my heart pumped in adornment for you

Visions of love and of companionship

All my desires revolved around you

My body fervently explored your false truth

I thought I had found what I wanted most

But in reality it was all a hoax

Screaming for your affection

My life lost its upward direction

My child was neglected dare I fail to mention

You lied, rejected me

I'm disappointed

I'm overwhelmed and resentful

Wasn't living I was dying

Chasing your reciprocation of love and affection

The skies have spread open

I see Heaven!I’m still alive

I'm still here one day at a time

You were hoping I would die

Persistent efforts made to delude and discourage me

To keep me restrained

Attacking my will to fight

I begged you to bring me to oblivion

I pleaded every night

I lost anyone who has ever loved me

Because they couldn't bear see you by my side

There was a time and a place

You and I once shared space

I yearned for your kiss, your touch your embrace

All I wanted was relief but all you gave me was more pain

Your tainted memory lives on in the poems I create

I have conquered some demons alone

But your one I slay every day

Your dark existence lives in the cells in my veins

Rejection of your elusive affection

Regurgitated familiar emotions of self-hate

I choose life over your lies

I am grateful for all you have taught me

Just for today I am free

I won't shut the door on the pain

Which has fueled my efforts to change

My life is on support

I'm so grateful to see another day

A blessing inside a harsh lesson

A unmerited gift and curse

Through the divine I found hope again

After a once hopelessly fatal

LOVE.

Lonely Grief

I found my best friend

Someone I never wanted to lose

The twin to my flame

The lace in my boots

Still his presence in my life left my heart bruised

I was blind to reality he passed right by me

I believed his smooth words his actions reminded me

I never was never would be how could it be

I loved him more than he could ever love me

Now we stuck in a situation but who is beside me

It's hard to see the truth when I love so blindly

I feel so ashamed, put my feelings on display

Would die for a love but love lives in another place

My time is coming

They say true love is worth the wait

But what if the only one who would love me

Already passed away

So codependent so confused

Always left feeling deluded and used

So damaged inside for only one thing I'm good

I sometimes wish I was the kind of girl he liked

I could be another girl

The kind he pays attention to

I wanna smile, I wanna dance

God give me another chance

At life, at love at happiness and romance

Fill my soul, make me whole

Heal my scars every scratch

Bless me with redemption, help me forget my past

Pour favor over my loved ones

Replenish everything I lack

Ensure from here when I extend my love and devotion

I won't run off fumes, emotion or delusion and

It will finally find its way back.

Complicated Emotion

I cannot give myself to someone who cannot penetrate my mind

I must guard my heart and pick apart small talk as

I read between every line

Things left unsaid; messages unread

Feelings so tense, thoughts ruminate in my head

I get confused, none of it makes sense

I cannot submit without giving my permission

I'm in my head

I'm in my heart

Over the rainbow floating among the stars

So, I retreat mentally, even though his frequency

Pairs with my energy I give him everything

I'm silly but I feel like he was meant for me

I am weak with vulnerability strength is my essence

I have never needed a man

So used to flying solo

Beat of my own drum to my own dance

There have been others who have tried to tame me

That didn’t last

It takes a special kind to infiltrate my mind

He is not the one for me

But the memories of this thrill will last a lifetime

I give him what I have and right now he gives me what I need

I receive his firm guidance and act accordingly

This can’t get much deeper than the still waters

In which we splash so freely

He ignites a fire in me I thought was long gone and extinguished

I’m bent over on my knees, and he is all I can see

Doing silly things that don’t make sense to me

He sees who I am and it feels like

I am a queen in his adoration

I am over my head in feelings

I scream his name with angst, knowing deep down inside

the end game has its season

I still drop everything when he tells me he needs me

I do what I’m told; truth be told

He drives me crazy with satisfaction

I am his “good girl”

Wrapped in the grips of this rare attraction

Maybe I love him?

I’ll do anything to make him happy

Whatever it takes it doesn’t matter

We make one when we unite

However,

I am the lonely one when you subtract him.

Discontent

So much pent up resentment lingering in silence

Lust masquerading as love

Drenched in fantasies of vengeance and violence

I was just trying to be honest, not suffer in silence

Causing strain on the first love I'd felt in a while

Was not what I was seeking

My feelings were hurt and that's being modest

Longing to be everything you said you felt for me

But that's just nonsense; A lofty concept

We don't see things the same way

When you stole my heart I remember the day

And then there was a brink in reality

You have too much on your plate

In between a rock and hard place there is no real room for me

No time, no place

Should I dare to voice a desire

It's met with anger and hostility

You see attention seeking with tears streaming down my face

I'm just trying to figure out my place

I thought we were family

Lately when I think about us all I feel is anxiety

I'm a scorpio, you can't lie to me

I allowed you to penetrate my heart and mind,

You became a king in my eyes

Your throne was my safe spot

All I want is a fresh start

Sometimes I want to walk away and never look back

All I wanted was to feel your love again

But you cut me off from that

Trust is broken tears and grief

We all say and do things sometimes when we are upset

Things we feel but may not mean

I shouldn't hold it against you, but you hold it against me

Healing isn't a linear journey

The truth sets us free ! Love is all we need; Reciprocity

I have been so down for you but

I am always an inconvenience when it comes to anything I need

It's been a long time since I felt like a priority

Lately I feel like a minority

When everything I do is from the heart, for the majority

But what do I do when there is no more use for me?

When you only hear my cries as nags

And you push farther away from me

I don't have alot to offer but what I have

I considered yours I don't know what this is anymore

My heart aches to be sure

To be secure, to grow and learn the ones I love

To be better than we were

Love is a tricky thing

I don't want to leave I want to stay

I just don't want to feel this way

Like I mean less to you than you do to me.

Volume II:

Familial Ties/Societal Plights

(Side A) “Nostalgia & Homage”

Words

Sometimes, when you feel you have nothing to offer anyone in the world, your family or yourself, and God has no use for you the universe sends you an angel (or two, or three). Messengers and protectors that deliver a fraction of inspiration that penetrates youin a way that refuels your efforts to live and gives you a sense of hope. They propel you into a state of light where there was only darkness and gloom.

I mean no disrespect when I say this, but I am personally not religious at all. At least not in the dogmatic sense. However, spirituality and my journey with it is special to me. I cannot denythat there is power greater than myself that works in my life and always has.

I feel like one of the most beautiful things I have experienced when I am connected to my higher power is being connected and feeling guided and protected although I cannot always define that power.

It is not by my grit or wit that I have made it out through impossible situations, found hope after feeling void of it or completely hopeless.

I believe there is a power greater than what I can perceive, that loves all of us, you and me equally. My journey has propelled me torealize this. Who am I to say there is no God? I may not be well versed in ritual, religion or practice but I am a grateful believer.

Motherly Love

My rock when life hit bottom,

My gasp for air when I was drowning

You would think her a God of sorts the way that sounded however,
Every time I lost myself her prayers helped to find me

When the woes of life compounded, she counted her blessings

Tears in silence

Chaos pursued

Though, her faith was firm and grounded

Her flesh made her fallible life made her malleable

Her work propelled her efforts to make

Our life as manageable as possible

Born in difficult times she struggled and fought

To give me a better life

Confident but not full of pride, rarely boasting

A true Queen works behind the scenes in humility

When no one knows it

I love her, a woman full of love

I feel like God hand-picked her for me

But that was never enough

A thousand times she lost her only child

In the rhythm of sex, rock-n-roll and self-destruction

A mother's love touches everyone

They may clock out at the job, but their work is never done

Frightened in the night when things were just not alright

Only to rise with the sun to "get things done"

Her essence is grace I would trade anything

To go back and cherish and save our old memories

Time flies by and regardless of the silent tears

She has cried; she never gave up on me

She told me to "never stop fighting", "follow my dreams"

And "never stop learning"

"You can be anything you want to be"

She is a perfectly imperfect human being Always true to herself

And kind to everyone she meets

A true friend, mother, sister, and grandma indeed

For all she has been to me

I am thankful eternally

My prayer is that one day she'll be proud to know

Her prayers were heard in the clouds

To know she is seen, heard and held with high regard

And that this life won't be in vain because we have come so far

Rubie's and diamonds are a girl's best friend

But when you are broken and hurting

Your needs and wants seem very different

And although I have struggled much

And hit many brick walls,

Stumbled, and seemed a lost cause

My mother never changed her number

In case that desperate day

I needed her

I would call.

Grandma (Memories)

Memories of way back then

It's like yesterday to us when grandma first touched our hands

We stood together as a unit

Blood running through the veins of her strong black praying hands

Nothing could divide us because together we would stand

Grandma has been the pillar of strength to catch us when we fell

She had so much hurt and regret yet by the looks of us

And her home the unkeen eye could never tell

You could tell grandma your secrets

And if asked she'd say you never rang her bell

Her eyes carried the tears of generations

And decades you could call them a wishing well

Year after year, storm after storm

My grandma left a legacy that will continue to carry on

In the midst of adversity she taught us to always stand tall

She told us to have no fear but God

She was the bravest of us all

This is not a time for crying, this is not a time for sorrow

For my grandma would always remind us

"Joy always comes tomorrow"

We shall rejoice in her beauty and her presence not wallow

Although we can all acknowledge

She is not physically here any longer

Don’t let that weigh you down my family

We all know she loved and lived

A FULL life a long and pleasant existence

We have to remember what she taught us and cheerfully reminisce

This world has never met one like her

We have been truly blessed by her

Her dedication, valor, strength, love and persistence…

This world has never met one like our precious little lady

And won’t since.

She Stood Tall (4'11)

She stood tall; even at 4'11

She stood tall even on the day she went to heaven

She stood tall even when the odds were against her

She stood tall for she knew her Father above was always with her

She bore life into those who crossed her path

On a good day she would cry in isolation

Yet burst out with a genuine laugh

She peeled the onions, washed the clothes,

Prepared and paid the bills

She didn't care for dishonesty, Tom foolery or cheap thrills

She was a woman of stamina, integrity and honor

She had friends and tons of family

Who loved and admired her

This world has taken a loss but she no longer has to carry her cross...

When approaching our lady with nonsense

You might just want to stop and pause

She taught us self-respect

Things we haven't learned yet

But if you asked her about her life she wouldn't have many regrets

Her love and her devotion made us all who we are

She gave her life for us to survive

And though we didn't always see it

She only meant to teach us about life

She was a cook of all connoisseurs

Her kitchen held open doors

You came to her house hungry

But you always left physically and spiritually full

Our lady has now passed from the latter years

Of darkness into divine light

And from above inside the stars

She will continue to twinkle bright.

Grandma's Hands (Memories-Remix)

Memories way back then

Remembering when grandma first touched my hand

We stood together as a unit

Blood strains of strained generations running through the veins

Of beautifully worn praying hands

Nothing could divide us

At the roughest times our family stands

I see you in my dreams

We all dream to see you again Grandma

Been the pillar of strength to catch us

Although many times we still fell

We didn't have much we always had enough

At the looks of us you couldn't tell that our life was a bit to handle
Sometimes; times were real rough

Grandma.

Secrets rested in her; always SAFE

You never gave up on me as reckless as I seemed to be

The glue that held our family; Grandma

In the midst of adversity we saw you would always stand tall

The most horrific nights told us to have no fear but God

Grandma

The bravest of us all

This Is not a time for crying

No time for sorrow

You would always remind us

"Joy always comes tomorrow"

Rejoicing in your love

All that remains

All that was

Grandma

The softest grip of the strongest hand

I continue to hold on.

For Brie, Love Mommy

I got nothing left to lose

I just got everything to prove

When I wake up my first thought is always reuniting with YOU

You are my ray of sunshine

You are the joy in my glow

But they tell me that I am the reason

There is darkness in your shadow

I delivered you into this world

Still it seems at this point you may never know

That your life gives me motivation to fight

I've just been losing every battle in this war

I wish I made better decisions

I made so many choices that affect you deeply

Because now you are two parents below zero

Because of me your heart is bleeding.

Your tears shed because you never get to see me

You are the sparkled Unicorn

That comforts my storms and blesses me with a rainbow

You are the hope that keeps me hanging on in this painful existence

You are my love, you are my angel

I need for you to know that everything will be alright

When life presents itself to you

I pray you stand and fight

I'll never give up on us

Baby girl you are the bright side in my life

With every fiber in my soul I pray we reunite

Promise...Promise...Promise...

Everything will be alright.

Thoughts of Mama

In thoughts about my mama I get a smile on my face

When it comes all that have loved me no one takes her place

By my side every night hustled every day

I always had food to eat a place to lay my head

She never went out to the clubs, she stayed with me instead

And though I was a rotten child

She loved me despite that

I cried on the floor so many nights

She would gently rub my back

My emotions ran so high that hers lost their flare

She was left all alone

I feel I never deserved her loving care

Some rare nights she needed me, and I was not there

So ashamed

Not only did she carry her own

But my cross she's had to bear

Mom if your there I really want to say

I understand the time has long since passed

That you can hold my hand

I pray to God nothing was in vain that you have had to withstand

Mom, I thank you, I need you

Please don't forget about me, please don't be mad

I've been selfish and disrespectful

I wish I could take it all back

Mama, I love you and am grateful for your existence

I'm grateful for your enduring love

For your patience, for your commitment

Even If I never get to build you that new home on the hill

Never forget you kept me alive

I wanted to die on my own will

Morals and values you did your best to instill

I pray that we can know each other again

I pray our wounds heal

You didn't raise me to be a derelict and lame

I chose to use and I indulged in reckless games

Mom I am stronger,

I am wiser because of you

I am proud to say I have a phenomenal mother

I call her YOU

My daughter has a grandma and life

She can aspire to be and look up to

Your sacrifice has given me life in way more ways than birth

I know things will be different at this point

Because of the stress I've caused

Only hope you get to receive back

The many things you have lost

I pray for redemption for our lives

For the child we both lost.

Auntie-Final Words

Auntie - My heart and my voice will always make noise

And be mix of over the top personality wisdom and force

You told me it was okay to be exactly who I was

Because in this world you have no other choice

Rest well OG- We ALL love you.

Auntie -

One of the realest and gifted women

To walk down the streets of Broad and Olney even at night

When you were alive I could too! Why?

Because we walked side by side

Now that you have passed on

you remain one of the great females in our family

When it came to living, you "survived"

The "blue collar" vs "white collar scholar",

"Anything for a dollar holla" backward ass society.

Reminiscent and admiring your tough sovereignty

You may be physically gone but your presence is held strongly

This is an honest and overdue attempt

To sit and process this hit to my childhood

My memories all of which you have always been

All the vocabulary in the world isn’t enough to describe

My "Auntie" in any sentence

With all my gratitude love and respect my words

To you is a day late and overdue attempt to express

From the soul and define the *Legacy of Devotion*

that you are leaving behind

None could ever personify resemble or multiply

The amplified larger than life personality

Who seemed to never age much over time

Family -

We had our issues and we always found solutions

When you came through Family -

So large before passing by a cousin on the train

I'd be introduced to them by you:) Family -

I never told you I loved you enough

I lost my way and forgot what family love meant

Family - I had broken heart after heart and pipe dreams

And you reminded me when I was a girl to keep my head

And as a young woman I’m learning what you meant

I never told you enough how my heart miss you so much

I was a little stubborn and distance and time

Makes staying in contact rough

The last comment you sent was some beautiful emojis

You told me you loved me and now

I’m celebrating your life instead

We share genes of eternity in our family

Our history carries on a *Legacy*

Because each one of us has a piece

Of your wisdom and knowledge we are carrying

My mama reminded me we are never prepared for any loss.

no matter how expected or untimely

I don't want to say goodbye

Too many tears we all have cried

Every year it seems another loved ones "time"

I will just say I love you

Thank you for your role in our family and my life

Carol Denise, I will see you again

With all our family and friends

On the other side in love and light.

Aunt Cynthia-Final Words

My Aunt Cynthia; she is technically my older cousin, but you know how we do in black families. She was high in the ranks for me, so I called her my Auntie and respected and loved her as such. She never failed to show and tell her love to all her family, her daughters, grand kids, nephews, friends, and nieces including me. I will miss her as we all will. We are never ever fully prepared to say goodbye to anyone we loved dear and this is not goodbye just see you soon because she believed in God's love and she knows there is life after this one.

For my Aunt Cynthia:

She was fierce

A force to be reckoned with

She dealt with many obstacles along her journey

Yet she pressed on as if they didn't exist

She cared for herself, her family, her friends

One of the strongest women we have ever met

She never gave up, never gave in

I remember like it was yesterday when she stood up for me

If you knew her you would know

She was sweet as pie but full of fury

Mess with her family and that's the end of your story

She gave God all the glory

Worked hard all her life and made lemonade out of water

I wish I had been there more for her

I pray she knows how much she meant to all of us

That she was held in high regard and adored

It's not easy being a black woman at any age

She wore it with style and grace

She may have been hard on us

Because of the strife she faced everyday

But my Aunt loved and she loved hard

And she can never be replaced

I love you. Rest easy Queen.

We all love you and will cherish your memory.

Advice 3x

All of us in life have experiences that leave us bewildered

in the moment and clear as day in hindsighT

They told me when I was young

To "never let the same snake bite you twice"

Lessons are to be learned and not repeated

To my friend reading this that I've never met

This is my first hint of advice

Beware vicious snakes

They lie in the grass waiting and lurking for an unassuming prey

Do not fall into the rat trap

Run for your life, towards freedom and safety

Like a slave chasing hope on the underground for a better life

I have almost drowned in tears of hurt, but haven't we all?

Fallen and stumbled ripped apart, tooth and claw

Praise God, for I survived many lions dens

And made it out alive; no scratch, no bite

However, I am forever scarred

Take it from me take what I am saying seriously

Stray away from traveling into places you don't belong

If you desire to have a friend, you must learn to be one

In order give and respect love,

You must learn how to see it and receive it

Love without fear

Love without motive or selfish gain

And share it with someone who may really need it

Never can we quite measure the effect we have had on another's life,
How they felt we treated them

Do right by others and Karma will be in agreement

The world can be a big scary place

Hostile and cruel, depending on how one perceives it

But try your best not to let society make you sour, or jaded

Things are subject to change, just as the seasons

Lifetimes can be short

Eternity is said to be forever

The heart cannot help or choose with whom it falls in love

What is love exactly? How do you do it?

Give it? Receive it? Prove it?

The answer is there, behind every action, every laugh, every tear

Temporary pleasures, thrills, vices and sex appeal

Are not enough to sustain self-esteem

When you are face to face with your own demons

Face to face

With the shadows that have haunted your thoughts at night

So my advice is to focus on the light

Where the darkness cannot hide and must subside.

Conscious Prayer

God, my creator, the Most High in the universe

I want to take the time to thank you for everything

And everyone in my life

For every gift you have given me

And all the generous ways you have shown up

Your strength carries me through when I feel I can't go on

The grace you have shown me is a gift

The mercy you have extended to me is beyond what I deserve

Oh I am so grateful,

So thankful for your protection and love

You have blessed me beyond measure

It is only through you that I am healing,

That I am finally starting to grow

There are so many things about life I failed to learn

Many opportunities I missed out on

You remind me that we all learn as we grow

To dust the past off and steadily push forward

Your forgiveness is already paid with your blood something

I cannot buy not a trophy I can earn

Without you I am a empty vessel sinking in murky water

Without you I have no assistance

In becoming a mother to my daughter

Without you my life has no meaning

The seeds planted in me have no water

Without you I am alone in this world

Without you I have no hope, I make poor choices

A Prisoner to self-will...participating in self-destruction

You are the essence of everything good in me

You turn my pain into purpose

The light in you expels the darkness that keeps pursuing me

I don't need religion to cultivate what you mean to me

I ask you for guidance and direction and you always lead the way

And though I have left a trail

Of disappointment, humiliation and pain in my wake

You have covered me in forgiveness

Intending good plans not disaster for me God

I am tired of letting myself and everyone down

I am tired of my old ways please change me from the inside out

Please teach me to love myself, to hold my head high

I'm tired of hanging it down

Please teach me how to live as an adult

I ask you for the willingness to be willing to do anything you ask

Creator, please tilt and straighten out my crown

Let my hands be clean and ready to lift someone else up

When they are down

Take the poison inside me and transmute it into medicine

Give me the courage to keep trying

Your will not mine

I trust you and your divine time Heavenly Father

My mother is a good woman and she loved me the best she could

Please forgive me for the hurt I caused her

I'd do it differently if I could

My baby girl is struggling and only getting older

My prayer is that you comfort protect and bless her

My family are all spread so far and wide

God please send them love and my gratitude

For being a part of my life

I have friends I may never talk to again

So help me be a better friend in honor of them

God bless everyone

In love and light.

Absolute

In life there are some ideas, situations and facts

That are absolutely black and white

Concrete, not up for debate,

Surely non-negotiable and completely finite

An example of that is one day we will all run out of time

We may not get a chance to say goodbye

And every day we get to live is a day closer to the day we die

There is no extension there are no exemptions

It's a hard pill to swallow especially if you've found life unkind...

At some point we all wish we could press rewind

Try it again one more time the thought itself is sublime

However, there does exist a grey area

Where you can fully love or value a person and still be mad at them

Maybe even say some things you wish you hadn't said

When you can feel alone

Yet surrounded by a myriad of family and friends

The silver lining is that the best parts of your character were
Cultivated by mistakes you made back when

Some experiences repeated themselves

Some things you vowed never to do again

When betrayal stabbed you in the back

And harsh lessons came with blessings

The older you get the more you may understand about life

Still so many questions go unanswered and you come to realize

We are all on our separate journeys at the same exact time

There is no "perfect" human

And no one is doing everything right

There is no comfort in comparing your inner worth

To what someone else appears to have on the outside

Trauma and blame gets passed around and spread like cancer

Obstacles surely come and we trudge the best we can past them

We have been fed so many lies, the truth however cannot hide

Beauty is a currency in our society though, how do you measure and

Equate the value in someone's heart

Versus their waist and pretty face?

Sometimes the ugliest people

Are the most esthetically attractive

And have obtained monetary gain

Joy and pain come in temporary waves

And the absolute truth is

The most consistent factor of life is change

Courage is the avenger of fear and love is the antidote of hate

Troubles will come, and troubles will fade

And even if you stay the same

The world will keep on spinning anyway.

(Side B) "Perspective"

Words

Feeling completely out of balance. My heart is sad today. I feel the weight of beingincompetent as a parent. Sometimes I feel so alone. Most times I realize it does notmatter. I am used to having pieces of me scattered all around, shattered, and dismantled. I have left a lot of memories behind, but they left me scarred for life. I am too hard on myself people say, and I wish I felt like they were right but there isa battle inside that I fight. It is hard sometimes to make it through the night.

I will be alright.

My thoughts and emotions get so overwhelming at times, so I cry, and Iwrite and give life another try. These are some thoughts I have on days where I second guess my worth and allow the past to consume my present moments, stealing the blessings the here and now brings. I am profoundly grateful, after every ten steps I fell behind I move forward two and grow a little more. I was told recently "the journey is the destination" and "there is no race to get there." That spoke to my heart. It is all about perspective. I have to remind myself it is okay to not be okay at times and that feelings always pass. I am not my thoughts or my past.

Unity Aligned

Gracefully I walk away

Old days trenches, empty spaces

Leaving an impression never any traces

Was lost, found my life surrounded by Divine graces

Into the unknown my soul travels the dark nights

To my souls aligned sacred places

I do not regret the past

It is the essence of what I am made

Carry the pain in my backpack

And trudge ahead to better days

My shadows so many days urged me to numb the pain

Insane

Ready Fed up

Face to face

One by one slaying the demons angry at the love that is me

Spitting out nothing but hate

Respect! That's the name of the game

Game over

Answering the call speaker phone in my zone

We are collective, never alone

Every reflection you see should remind you of the

ABSOLUTE TRUTH WE ARE ONE

I will no longer be quiet You can no longer silence me

I am. We are.

The people transmuting darkness bearing light

The UNIVERSITY

Respecting the shadows

Illuminating frequencies channeled beyond the stars

Transformed from 3D Pain

Reminds me to appreciate my blessings- Change

Disinterested in the extremities of washed up days

The truth of my being dissipates as I sage and

I shake old paradigms and faulty beliefs

Souls across the globe waking up to see

Everything I needed is IMPRINTED

Within the core of my being

Proof.

I've learned some lessons

My ego speaks so loud I can’t hear my spirit

I hear a Divine whisper; humble surrender

Meet me with low vibrations rage.

I will render

Spread love in my surroundings

I will cherish you Forever.

We are all but one yet uniquely made

We must remember

This is not our home destination

Every one of us was sent here to raise creations vibration.

Black Lives Always Matter

So, now Black Lives Matter?

I just turned off CNN picked up my pen

Took a break from social media

So I could have some peace within

Superficial fads, political trends

Aw shit wait a minute! "URGENT Message! THIS JUST IN!"

Black Lives Matter Movement: Whoa I didn't know

Should I raise my fist?

Hop on the bandwagon and cruise with this

Because up until this "old news" trend

Being Black and a Black Female in this or any generation

Hasn't really been worth its weight in privileges

Unless you shined some shoes and paid some dues

Or survived by grit and silent harsh truth

We shall overcome in time; All lives should matter equally...

But I do not think they do

Intellectually Placated Racially Stigmatized

Sexually degraded in any man's eyes:

Be it color, status, secrets, fantasies lies

Still a slave wearing different chains of the invisible kind

It took 2020 vision to help me recognize

Black Lives Matter?

Yes, that is a question not a statement to me

I don't see how any lives matter in this society

I must have missed this

Women like Tomi Lahren and Kim Kardashian

Are the reason my suicide was almost a success

Seeing the vast shame I already felt for being a different race

Economic status, shape size or breast

Until this year anyone who was melanin deficient said

Racism was "a thing of the past and

Was not relevant in their "blind eye"

Statistics and logistics want me to be violent

Loot a store; Be labeled a whore...

Be a liar and poor OR

Become an athlete/Vixen/ Bunny Ranch Kitten/

Rap star if you wanna make more

What the fuck am I even fighting for?

At this age I have existed in the trenches

Gracefully accomplishing almost every statistic

Try raising your vibrations in a diverse dimension

Addictions

Afflictions Resentments Mental Illnesses

Interpersonal Conflictions

Hard won gained experience and hope from seeing the corrupt

Systems and mental prisons we ALL exist in

If you see me as a threat because I am Black

Take a long gaze

I am a mirror to reflect your HATE right back

Fear is the ROOT and cause of all that

Why do Black Lives Matter now all of a sudden

They did not matter when we were afforded

Different statuses and privileges based on COLOR

Why does my black life matter now

When you did not want to be my friend

Why should I pump my fist roar my voice

And viciously ignite my pen

For a highjacked cause that is just used as a tool or scapegoat towards
A REAL LIFE MATTER

That damn sure did NOT matter "back" then

When I was only a sex toy fetish to your neighborhood playboy

Always considered "less than

When I was only ever the (token black girl) to even out the photo

To any of my non- colored friends

When I almost lost my DIVINE confidence

In self harm and targeted hateful attempts

Labeled (proud arrogance)

Why did not my Black female life matter back then?

Bullied in School for more than my color and skin

In a district and Nation I am not really welcome in

Sorry this Beautiful Black Female has had it

That's what's in

I'm standing up but not for society's entertainment

Karma is a pretty lady we all kiss once or twice

Its this generation and she is patiently waiting

We must UNITE

I'd rather be a hermit choosing my battles practicing discernment

Than "Keeping up with the Joneses"

Than biting my tongue until its bleeding and numb to give the

Satisfaction to people who only acknowledge INJUSTICE

When its comfortable for them

I am a friend I am a mother I am a HUMAN

I am the Phoenix

Scorpio is my Sun

Rage and passion my assailants

Karma is the justice that every resonated shiver in my ink

I pray provokes it on every injustice

Serving the Most High Divine

My wings clipped for purpose.

We shall fly, no more sailing coast to coast

Let me reintroduce myself

I am Indya Renee

Black a little Irish and Cherokee Female

Whose done with this societal hypocritical BULLSHIT

I am A Life like yours, we are more similar than distant

ALIVE and because of that I am worth it

Remember me

Female or not Black Yellow Blue or not

Equally I have a right for speech and Existence EQUALLY as a

HUMAN BEING All life SHOULD deserve it.

(but does not)

I can see my inner child she's screaming

"GET OUT" Hide Run from the BS

Do you remember her?

Placated her with kindness and gas lit her false love and teachings

Dragged out all her mistakes?

So much so she kept her head down

Confused between worlds and paradigms

But starting to figure shit out

LOVE

The only answer to sum up all equations LOVE

Sees no color, status, dynamics ages, sizes or hatred

LOVE THE antidote to UNIFY and CONSOLE

HATE begets Hate and only ends up in WAR

She knew ashes would rise in her eyes as she burned in the fire

Speaking a truth that she hopes would inspire

Like the Sage she smudged around.

She left in the night

Like a slave chasing freedom in the underground

Fighting for ALL LIFE.

TIME BOMB

Tick, tick, tick

The sound of my beating heart

A ticking time bomb, destruction lies

I'm a push to start my words a self-fulfilling prophecy?

Nah, it's just art

My words penetrate the hate infiltrates

But love carries me since I cannot walk

I am but a bomb waiting to tick lyrics waiting to spit

A fist waiting to hit

A hand held out waiting to get A casino waiting to bet

A chair waiting to sit

Tick, tick, tick Click, click, click

I am not a gun I am the tip at the end

What is life without strife what is a blade without the knife What would wrong be if there was no right

What colors can you see if your eyes are shut wide

I been sleep all my life

My eyes squint at the light waking up to reality

Screaming on the inside

Confusion and ignorance submerged in lies and false pride

Love meant nothing Love was a lie

Love was denied Love saved my life

To love and lose is better than to hate and get by

She was a gift from the God up above

Precious cargo she is pure as a dove

The only experience I truly felt loved

Was in her heart in her warmth

I felt like someone

The sadness in her eyes I can't help but to cry

I don't wanna die, I wanna be right by her side

Everything is alright promise she'll be alright

Wolves can cry I cried so many times

Now lost in the gap between left and right

A broken record

A lost sheep

A motherless child

Blessings, blessings, blessings

Thank you I'm still alive

Thank you for another chance

Thank you for not leaving my side

Words and intent

I misused them a lot

I had no idea till now how much my word has power

86 that writing that says I'll end a tragic life

Because I am not enough for the Christians or the nots

I don't have enough knowledge to dissect and fall in line

So being still I will

I know my God is on my side

Love I don't know Love I don't show Love I need to live Love I want to give

I am not afraid...but Lord I am dismayed Confusion had me stuck

Doing the same things over again

Now they know my name I do not want this fame

I do not do not want to play these games

Word

Mine means nothing Heart

Still the same status

A fallen child jumped head first into change

Who deceived the grave

Begging to be saved

No one is coming to save me no one wants to play

Cards. Been dealt. Been folded. Been raised.

Some laugh at my downfall

Some give God praise

I'm still here for some reason

Taking life day by day

Tainted and now jaded but my heart's still the same.

Segregate Hate

Spent lifetimes, hours, days giving misguided praise

Pushed my dreams aside on hopeless nights

Only to wake early mornings and

Harvest someone else's in the day time

Admitting myself once again to a mental prison

With no way out in sight

Rested on the bay till my playtime was docked

We set up to hit rock bottom more than any jackpot

Many days on tours as a naive girl

Sold to the confinements of ridicule and stigma

Caught in the crossfire of 2 wards

The Beautiful The Elite

Don't know they are the sheep

They can't empathize with love, honesty or integrity

They don't understand trial and tribulations

Nor what it's like to be free

That must be why they can treat us all

With such disdain and attempt to enslave the light

And love in you and me

Golden Kissed Melanin My skin

My society conditioned me to be ashamed of it

I unapologetically and eloquently say these words...

We can STILL RISE and be GRATEFUL

I am proud of my Heritage and

Earned the right to say I am American

Rage in my blood as my skin and razor touch

The hands were dealt; now the jig is up

We all been used, abused but 100 years passed

And we still got chains holding US

War on Color War on US

War on HATE WAR on LOVE?

I wanted to have hate for the sex I never agreed to give up

I had to forgive the crime against my innocence

Molestation is something that may never be healed

But is always learned

Dark and Light White, Yellow, Brown Black Red

History, Karmic Lessons How does Human Race Sound?

We are not the same

DNA is subject to change

Can we Bring back humility and hugs?

If we are gonna divide and set things aside

Can we UNIFY all walks of life

Marching side by side and segregate hate.

EGO TRIP

This whole life been a trip

Driven towards destruction with the hands of the wheel my EGO

Labeled crazy, insane, weirdo, evil

Pills fed for the brain that never killed the pain

Unmanageability in the place of love, hopes of stability

The cheapest of thrills ensued to get me killed

We wanted so much for me to die, guess it isn't time

Thankful, God's Will

There seems to be another way

For my mind and heart to change

For the old haunts and taunts to redeem another's fate

(hopeless as myself)

Seems I wasn't alone on the fast lane

We so wearily pursued oblivion on the highway that led to our grave

There is a way out

It ain't in no pill

There is a way to love

It ain't in no cheap thrills

I am not a morally void woman

Mother or child I harbor a disease with no cure

The ladder to spirituality carries me upward

And out.

Pain Undone

Prayer and silence

from my tongue transforms my degradation to character

Defects, undone

Victory won; Gratitude in my heart

Triumph to a victorious finish

The end of a seemingly futile, hopeless start

Inspires the melody in my song

Encourages Karma to forgive my wrongs

Fears and weaknesses evolve wisely to courage and strength

Illusions, delusions and paranoia dissipate

Into reality as my spirit awakes

Love and hope for a new season

WE shall Overcome

You better believe it

Long have I perceived myself to be infected

Neglected, unprotected; persistently rejected

Failed to be anyone else, never satisfied with my own reflection
Promises fulfilled I never manifested

Responsibility I eluded, responsibilities I never accepted

Honesty, willingness and an open mind

The fiber of grit, the grain the foundation of a

Higher Sources glory, individual testimony

From a life of misguided, traumatized,

Dereliction, self destruction…being unkind

They say joy comes in the morning one day at a time

Success is measured not by the arrival of vertical destination

But the sweat of traveled miles

Time is a gift and not a threat

A gratitude to speak of loud

I fear what lies on the other side of change

However the alternative is death or more pain

I have got to get through the mess to pass along a message

No longer place excuse or blame for my choices

It never was effective

Resulting in ripple effects with my insidious disease

Ego-searching for selfish gain and attention

I have got address correct and amend them

I have been afflicted

I am someone who lives with a disease that seeks instant-

Healing instant gratification and will search the floor

For more and find myself defeated

I find solace in the arms of surrendered

Warriors of this same plight

They found their strength, the antidote they say

When they "put down childish ways"

They ceased to fight

The only guarantee that it will work for me

They say would succeed

Telling the truth taking nothing from my fellow man

I live my life trusting a loving power

My trust in His care that I come to understand

That I commit just for today to live a different way

Become today better than I was then

And if time presents itself by grace

If I am willing to go to those lengths

I am blessed to keep what has been gifted to me

Having the awakening

The point is not for my prestige

Or self centered redemption

Yet freely give it away.

Mercy and Grace

He wrapped his arms around my weighed down shoulders

Told me that the hurt was over

He knew I had lacked any type of faith

He assured me I wouldn't stay in this hopeless place

I found comfort in his loving arms

I had searched for love in others yet barely found none

A wretch I am, a wretched sinner

He said "I've loved you since the very beginning"

I loved you when you lost

I loved you when you were winning

I loved you when you did right

I loved you when you were sinning

His love and mercy gave me ease and comfort

He gave me courage to push even farther

He crept into my soul and healed my scars up

I am the child He is my father he gave his son up

I have done some unthinkable things

So much guilt and shame God told me he's forgiven me

I wept for nights and days he wiped my tears from me

My veins were bound by endless chains

His power and grace has set me free

So many times I felt so alone

No house, no home to the streets I would roam

Wondered for years if joy would ever come

I searched for love in all the wrong places

Which is why I never found none

The joy is in His word

He's gifted me with a spoken word for the testimony

And redemption I claim

Is one that must be heard

I am a child of the one True God

I was a born sinner in this world

He lifted me up from the ashes

I was told I had a purpose in this world.

Bigotry

I could be gay, fat, or black

and the ignorance and hate in a bigot

would find a problem with that

I could be Korean or Chinese, from a far away country

Have a different ethnicity and in their eyes it would be all bad

I could have an abortion

Have more than one girlfriend or boyfriend

And be condemned to hell and back

To say the least, people with these beliefs feel that

People like me don't deserve respect, kindness

Or common decency

My hair may be short or won't grow

I could be super wealthy or impoverished and poor

On government assistance and sagging my pants low

And the judgements of my character

Would never measure me humanly equal

My skin makes me an enemy in their eyes

I am weighed out as fat when I may just be a little overweight

And what matters most is what's inside

Nappy hair and welfare minimum wage jobs

Slang you can't understand

Systemic enslavement that lasts a lifetime

Societies standards can tear good people down

It's hard to be your authentic self

When the world around you is so shallow

I could be a man in love with another of the same sex

They would burn me on the cross

And be righteously satisfied with that

Bigotry reveals itself in so many ways, it shows up in all shapes

And sizes and only reinforces disdain and hate

Day by day it is a poison infecting our environment

A mental pain that's so deeply engrained

In hateful men and women in our society

Affecting everyone silently.

Skin Tones

They say "beauty isn't only skin deep"

I say that should include every size, every shape, gender and ethnicity

Some crave to be a lighter shade

While others look upon their skin tone with

Disdain wishing their color would fade

Why do most of us this day and age

Struggle to love and embrace our unique authenticities

The way we were made?

We alter and pick apart but fail to look at the heart

And compare ourselves never measuring the same

In the summer sun the kisses

From its' rays glisten and gloss on some

While leaving the rest of us burned and flaked

Terribly painful for the rest of us

Snowy and white,

Tan & cool

Brown and mahogany too, midnight and caramel

Along with olive-

A variety of beautifully diverse hues…

Swirls and blends men and women

We all bleed the same no one is “less”

No one is “better than”

Every pattern of the rainbow has a story to tell

A song to sing, a dance to dance

Color identification and discrimination

Does no justice to the character and soul

The journey someone has walked

or the universal God that loves us all.

Royalty

A crown dented a bit, tilted, falling yet never touching the ground

It is my ancestor's plight, slaving in the day ceaselessly

Fighting for freedom in the night

My grandmother's prayers

My mother's hope for a better life

My daughter when she smiles and dances all alone

The purity of her heart and the innocence in her eyes

The tainted blood running through my veins

Sam Cooke's melody of the day that will surely bring change

My bloodline; their strength, true grit,

Their faith of God's mercy and grace

Tears in the dark, songs of praise in the day

Melanin hues within my skin specs of gold in my eyes

The will to keep on fighting

When all you can do is pray and cry

Moisture on the pillow from the pain in both eyes

Angels on every side battle scars that fade over time

Divine protection against every obstacle and all odds

Redemption and restoration of broken dreams and hard lives

Inspiration Divination

Family relations spread across the nation

Ties that bind

Favored by the Most High

A bloodline of survivors

Lemons made the lemonade we sweetened and sipped

as our heads held high

Royalty.

The Importance (of Loving Yourself)

When everyone left; I was left with myself

So now I am learning to become my best friend

"No one is ever going to hurt me like that again"

I refuse to be stuck

I gave way too much, it was never enough

My cup ran so empty, refilled it with all the wrong stuff

I became a nuisance, so ashamed of who I had become

It may take some time (as it heals all wounds)

Even though I am borrowing mine, I am battered and bruised

A lone wolf: nothing left to lose and no one to prove it to

The crook in my smile is reminiscent of the chemical clouds

I sought out in escape from the torment that followed me around

Growing to love the imperfections

I hated about myself as a child

When I'm loving and kind to myself

no one else's opinion counts

Solo ranger

Free spirit Flower child

Reminiscing on the youth that almost jaded me

Appreciating the lessons I'm learning now

I don't wanna sink in this sea of sharks

Even though I have let myself down

I won't let myself drown

No one save me, no rescue mission can fix it

I am the key, the way to succeed

It all lies within me

Speaking my truth makes some people so uncomfortable

But I will no longer be silent

My voice may shake but what comes out will be loud

I am not my past, it doesn't define me now

Divine love lives inside me and has carried me

From darkness into the light

Finesse

"Spin around, let me see how you fit in that dress

Just wanna make sure you look you're best"

Maneuvering through life with careful skill

Minimal effort zero regrets

My goal is to reap all the benefits

Discarding any obstacles in my path

Leaving behind any scraps

"Yeah, mmm I like the vision and how it all comes to fruition

Happiest when my needs and wants connect and are met

When it comes so easily, although I'm willing to put the work in"

"I want my cake, I want to eat it too"

"I like team players who follow my rules"

"It's no sweat I love full breasts, and good sex"

"But nothing compares to commas on a thick check"

"Look back at me, make it clap

No going back…you cool with that?"

"If you need some inspiration"

I got a cure in my pants for that"

"Say less," silver tongue pillow chat

"Finesse on my breath, no sleep, no naps, no time for that"

Casino bets- Private sex

Life's a gamble, take the risk see what happens next

"Gotta be quick on the draw, gotta think quick"

Left hand - Right hand

They have no business in communicating no making plans

They don't need to know what the other is doing

"That's how I get down"

"I like the splash and drip,

Wet like the ocean, I want to drown in it"

Bank rolls - Naughty clothes

A little blue cheese for the salad a snack for the road

Keeping every "square" in my circle, on a "need to know"

Planting seeds to watch them grow

"I can manage on my own but, its lonely when your solo

And I don't like to be alone

That's why I need two phones, one for "business and home"

And one for the "hustle and all my side hoes"

A man like me must always be in control"

Delicate words, whispers meant to "subtly encourage"

The agenda I have thought up

"Don't get in my way, but give me what I deserve

And I will give you what you "earned"

You will learn it's called "teamwork"

Everybody gets their time to shine

I see so much potential in you, let me borrow your light

So I can brighten mine

It's totally fine let's not waste any more time

It's valuable just like money so let's hustle and grind

Remember you are "special"

My number one

My favorite concubine.

Love (as a person)

She gives the warmest hugs

Always remembers the little things

Never keeps tracks of past mistakes

Hurts or grudges for too long

Built to last forever

She makes every simples things in life appear so much better

She is a rainbow and she shines after the stormiest weather

She is a protector

Her essence is pure there is no amount of fear

Or hatred that can affect her

Never superficial No profit to gain

She is more than a conqueror

She withstands all heartache, pain and tribulation

Anyone can see that she will never fade away

She is a constant among the times that consistently change

Comfort in the night, wiping away fears and tears from each eye

She is not struggle or strife

She is loyal support and endurance by your side

Patient and strong

Honest at all costs

Deceit and vengeance conflict with her

She brought me back to the light

The darkness had consumed me

Such a horrid sight

She held my hand and rocked me on each side

Whispering in the most nurturing voice

"Everything will be alright"

She is prayers to over come

Laughter when you need some

Selfless acts of kindness

And thankless deeds shared with anyone

Her fragrance smells like heaven

She is more than "happily ever after"

She is healing from heartbreak grief and loss

Remembered birthdays on the calendar

All we really need

More than a best friend

A wife, mother sister daughter and niece

A dad, brother, uncle, partner and husband

No conditions or limits

Healthy boundaries

The sweetest of memories, lessons learned, self-esteem

Our highest good, our motivations

And dreams of who we can be all start with all that she is

All that is she

LOVE.

Volume III: Evolution (Side A)

"Hopeless to Hopeful" (Mash-up)

Words

I find myself in doubt many times when I receive an accolade or compliment of any kind and coyly respond with a blushing “ah thank you BUT…” or “ I appreciate it BUT I could have done better” or “thanks but I have gained so much weight, need to hit the gym…” or “my smile could be better I need to fix my teeth”. Whatever the case may be inside I truly want to own it and receive it like I already know but something inside me recoils in doubt and insecurity, probably due to a low self-image and insecurity from my past trials and struggles with how I view myself in the outer world.

Why is it so hard to believe, receive and own that someone thinks I am pretty? Beautifully shaped or unique? That despite my struggles and past shortcomings that I am a good mother? A worthy person or gifted soul? Why is it okay for anyone else in the world to make mistakes and still be loved and valued but not me? When will my confidence and self-esteem not fall prey to past mistakes, failed relationships, missed opportunities, failures, traumas, or pain?

I am on a journey to discover and recover the answer not the “why am I not?” worthy or valuable of forgiveness, redemption, love, or success…but “why not?”.

All in my head

Was it all in my head

Was my mind just playing games

I give my all my love to those who can never reciprocate

I had love once the angel of death took him away

Tried to fill the void that was left

Chaos almost took me to the grave

So damaged; So lost

Still trying to find my place

Wrong time, wrong face State to state

Been broken into pieces blood shattered onto the floor

Mind laced with images of men who never wanted more

It's like I exuded dangerous territory

Heart crushed by those I adored

Had hopes of a fairytale

Life's been more like a horror

Praying my daughter has it better

I want so much more for her

All I want is love

Love is all I want

My baby she loves me; why isn't that enough

Hopes and dreams shot away by drugs and reckless fun

Feeling ill never be loved again by any one

Put myself on a shelf that's where I reside

In a house that ain't my home

All alone empty inside

So I cry and i write I write and I cry

I pray the angels find me

Cremate me when I die

Because I am a PHOENIX

From the ashes ill RISE Into a new creation

My wings will ignite the sky

Propelled by the pain that left such a stain

Tainted; Not Jaded

My heart never changed

I am just more aware of the games and now I play

Life handed me lemons

I made lemonade

And I'll never be picture perfect

I have few regrets all the lessons were worth it

People think I'm dumb

I know when true colors are showing

I'm smarter now; wiser

Not letting the past define me

Letting it mold me

Refusing to let the enemies control me

God does for me what I can't do for myself

I appreciate my scars and the heart that beats in my chest.

~Consequences~

Consequences of my actions

Caused a divine chain reaction

Every substance stopped working

Couldn't get no satisfaction

Try with the best intentions to get and stay quit

But chronically relapsing

They say if I want success

I gotta change things, people places, and perspective

I lost everything

Recovery and redemption is my only way past it

Self-will doesn't make sense

Sick and tired of living life like a homeless degenerate

Most days I wanna give up but I just can't quit

Its just I think how my daughter would feel

I hear her tears at night

She deserves better than this

My mom is sick and she's tired

Sick of me as it gets

Some days I wallow in shame like a lost tainted whore
And I'm the only one to blame
I did everything to escape the never ceasing pain
It only created more
Life made my heart sour as lemonade
Here let me pour some more
Begged for help in the fetal position
Face down on sinking floors
My liver is now as damaged as my soul
The choices I made were usually painfully poor
Acceptance is the key My Higher Power carries me
I'm a Phoenix meant to rise from the flames
Burning deep within me; I caused a lot of damage
I write out my pain with hope
That one day someone can relate
Someone can feel the depth of my soul
I write alone in the dark because my spirit needs healing
In fighting for my life
I will no longer conceal the real me

My little girl is hurting literally and figuratively

I thank God for not leaving my side

All the people who've been helping me

On this rollercoaster ride

Dismissing the gossip and the judgement ain't nothing left to say
Spreading love for all

For hate I'm truly lacking in the ability to let it affect me

I've cried myself to sleep

I still do most nights

Spirit died a couple times

With fake friends on both sides

My actions nearly lost me my family and friends

Divine love resurfaced within

Love unlike a man unlike the most euphoric high

Like is said I am a Phoenix

From the ashes I rise

I've done unthinkable things

I ask to be forgiven

I try to be better every day

Although sometimes I realize all I've experienced

I'm still here

Searching my purpose for my life

What is there left to lose

I'm on a mission before I die

To leave my daughter a legacy

For my mom's tribulations and trials.

Darkness to Light

Fresh out of the darkness crawling into the light of the sun

Felt like it was all over, really life has just begun

Swam in puddles of shame

Couldn't be trusted couldn't trust anyone

Addiction snatched any sanity I had

I was turned out and spun

Never thought I would go from honor roll

To a needle in my arm

Been yanked out of the mud because

Of this thing called LOVE

So many had love for me

But for myself I had none

Used people, places, and things

To change my feelings or escape them

Bounced around trying to find my way

My roots never grew in any soil

My track record says I'll get fail again

The last chapter in my life said it was THE END

Not alone, not anymore didn't realize

I wasn't way back then much more awakened

To the spirit and put my life in Divine hands

Been to hell and back

People talk they gossip, judge, and they snare

I hear the whispers I’m not crazy

But I cannot let them keep me in fear

The fact remains after all I been through

I’m grateful to still be standing here

God has a purpose it’s in His Divine plan

I don’t need to know details or figure it out

It doesn’t have to be clear

Its so warm resting in the light

So many times I wanted to give up

Still I continue to fight

Cried myself to sleep on so many nights

I felt like no one could understand my plight

I took to the pen, I’d cry, and I’d write

I'm still praying for stability and security

Freedom from pain and strife

Lately I make my own happiness

I’m just glad to be alive

I felt so alienated and outcasted from society,

So I lean on the few people that still walk right beside me

I am a Phoenix it’s in my blood

And from these ashes I rise

The creators on my side on my angels wings I fly

I'm sailing out of the absence of light into an ignited sky

I meet the heavens that glisten with every lost tear I've cried

When I'm doing the right thing good things don't pass me by

I will love again, and I will succeed all in due time

I’m grateful to know forgiveness I’m giving my best I’m trying

Situations that baffle me I don’t have run and hide

I have failed so many times,

As long as I have breath in my body

I am going to fight for my life

I’m free to be myself

I haven’t felt such hope in a while

Life been throwing me TKO punches

With my HP we throw them back round for round

I'm loving myself lately every curve, every scar

I'm loving me and every pound

They say I talk like a "white girl"

But I love how I sound

They labeled me crazy but still can't figure me out

I am not a diva; definitely not a bad bitch

I was lost, still finding myself out of the despair and sadness

It has been a long journey; I have just begun to smile again

I have goals and achievements I seek after

I am truly blessed and grateful for a chance

To make my life better.

Chronic Relapse

Now I'm at this place again it all fell apart

I should have known it would end this way before it even started

My daughter never sees me and as a mother I'm an imposter

I ran from love for so long that when I fell

I fell harder

I begged for his attention and now

I'm begging for redemption

The sickness in my veins harbors so much retention

I seek in all the wrong places to find some contentment

I begged for his attention

Now I’m begging to forget him

Praying that from this hamster wheel

I will finally stop spinning

Hoping that my loved ones will one day forgive me

Hopes to recover, mental conflicting thoughts that

I don’t deserve to live

My angel, my daughter doesn’t deserve me as a mother

I will never give up trying she doesn't have another

My mom won't be here forever to raise her

I need to step up, my daughter needs me to recover

I am scared and bound by these chains that linger in my veins

I've tried anything and everything there is to be addicted to

It's been the sum of my life and

I wonder if I'll ever change

Every year I'm starting over in a hopeless state

I stand in front of the mirror but I can't even look at my face

This is my plea for freedom my cry for relief

How could something that made me feel so good

Bring me to such a hopeless place

I'm ready ready to change

Ready for my place in this world

As the girl that the struggle didn't break

That rejection didn't phase

That her smiles she don't fake

That only prosperity, abundance, love and oneness

Are her birthright her destiny

I am not a bad bitch but I am a queen

I been blind for so long I just couldn't see

I want to truly thank from the bottom of my heart

The people that believe in me despite me unconditionally

I'm not gonna give up I never will

I have taken mad Ls

But by God's grace got back up every time I fell

I been a soldier ALL MY LIFE

Whether in heaven or hell

Bought many dreams sold some as well

All I know is today at this moment

I am grateful not to be dead

Arrested or buried 6 feet where I should dwell

I am a fighter

Gimme a cigarette and I'll light it

Let me get in my feels and you know I'll write it

There's nothing you could say that doesn't already haunt

me

I am my own worst critic, my worst enemy

I may be struggling right now but

I know in my heart it will be okay

I love the sunshine, but learning to dance in the rain

And when it hails

I sprinkle down some salt and PREVAIL

I may be in this place right now but not to no AVAIL.

Isolation

Alone in the darkness

Lights got shut off so I'm alone

Heartless in darkness

If only someone could love me to LIGHT

Love me to Fight;

Love me to LIFE

Love me enough to understand why I write

The painful scribes of someone who would rather die

Trying than live living to die

Trying to find love

Don't know if its above or down under

Really makes me wonder

What's the fine line between love and lust

What's the denominator between honesty and trust?

LOVE…LOVE…Me.

To writeTo fightTo life

To LIGHT

No way out

It took a while for me to see a way out

I been drowning in my sins

Been another month since I spent time with my child

Another year has passed and

I'm still drowning trying to find myself somehow

I fell in love with the feeling that it gave

Not knowing that the first hit might take me to my grave

It's life or death I’m a free woman

I never wanted to be a slave

Now I'm begging for someone to save me

For Gods mercy and grace

I used to hate my own reflection when I was a little girl

The only thing that has changed is

I'm not jaded by this world

I been left outcast, raped, molested and abused

To idols I ran to every time it was more than drugs I abused

Now I'm sitting here I got nothing left

Except the lions heart that is buried in my chest

I've stolen from the world

I've sold my soul by illicit sex

It seems as though my existence has resided

In the darkest trenches

I lost the love of my life when I was barely 21

When we fell we fell harder

Than the dawning of the sun

When they murdered him

Was when our life should have begun

My fairytale ended

I became turned out and spun

I'm just 11 days clean from heroin

These and comfort felt within the ccs may very well

Bring me to my end

So I write out these words to make it clear to you again

I'm not a bad person just an addict with a pen

My life is written but my story is not finished

Still I wonder what my life WHAT be like

If drugs had never been in it

If I had just made some better decisions

If my daddy had loved me back

If I could have chosen to forgive him.

Days Passed By

Seems as though all my life my days passed me by

Self-esteem so low I tried to cope

Having sex, creating chaos, and getting high

Most days I just craved to slit my wrist and fucking die

Sliced my skin, self-destructed

I caused so many tears in my mom's eyes

Reacting to my father's neglect

My spirit stared to fade at a young age

It's safe to say I had little self-respect

All my memories are laced with remorse and regret

A heart full of fear of the success

Future mistakes I would surely make but hadn't made yet

Traveled from state to state in hopes of finding a better way

Running from all my problems and pain, but at the end of the day

It was me I had to face

In this world I always felt so out of place

My solace was found in isolation

Men and various drugs and repeating patterns of insanity

I dreamt of being someone else all my life

Could never express the torment and confusion I had buried inside
With my head held down

I would cry and I would write

Cried myself to sleep, I was so lonely

I almost cried every night

My presence existed in the darkness there was no light

I was out my mind and strangled by strife

So green, so naïve

Learned so many things the hard way it brought me to my knees

No longer do I need to self-destruct

No longer do I need to run away

Learning to cope with life on life's terms isn’t the easiest thing

I am, however, grateful of every chance I get to learn

And to be a better person than I was yesterday

The emotions that I failed to face are ready to be healed and

I am willing to go to any lengths.

The Shadows

I resonate and appreciate the shadows

Shadows that dominate the night

A painfully beautiful sight

Thinking as my light is shrinking

Agony of the realization my thoughts are the shadows

When they are the manifestations of my thinking

I just cry and face my shadows alone in the absence of light

The words I write are just expressions of pain and hope

Simultaneously passing by

Tears Fears Years

After realizing all that matters has fallen through ever crack step

And been torn used and battered

I ponder the thought centered upon my absent self

Did my life even matter?

Matriculate

I am a matriculate of this new experience

My feelings arise and put me in a tail spin

I feel like I can't win

It all sounds good but doesn't make sense

I'm the one no one lays with

I'm the one who gets played with

I ruminate on hidden perspectives

Things that once felt so good and are ever changing

Maybe I shouldn't be complaining

On guard with my heart, restraining

As feelings of jealousy and isolation keep matriculating

It's not even the proper use of this word I'm saying

Maybe I shouldn't be complaining

My eyes are on the prize but something doesn't feel right

I gotta read between the lines

See things for what they are and how they fit into my life

I am a matriculate in the school of hard knocks

I could fail this class or graduate on the deans list at the top

What is my real place; Is it real or is it not

So distracted by my own thoughts

Anyways, I'm looking forward to brighter days

Goals and dreams that keep me motivated

Been sleeping in lately, my dreams have me feeling crazy

So I rest a little longer and then I feel like I'm being lazy

I will not stay stuck

I will fight for what I want

Won't lie, I miss the drugs

Escape from the pain of the past present and future

All that it is all that it was

I wish I had someone

Missing my family like I never had one

Don't get to close; I can't keep up

Pulling away because deep down I'm really hurt

Inspiration fuels my diversion of suicide

Lately I've felt so much joy

I just can't be happy all the time

I'm not the type

I need a little melancholy in my life

To remind me I'm not dreaming

I'm still alive

Ambitious matriculation placed me in a situation

Where I'm the odd fraction in a complicated equation

An orgasmic sensation

Building up my reputation

I am determined to revise my life's script and watch it grow

Into a beautiful matriculation.

Dreaming

I woke up today

A blessing to see the next day's Sun rays

Because nighttime is a fight for me

I am tired

I tried to take a nap (many recent nights before that)

Shook me to wake from my sleep

Futile to decipher the meaning behind the scenes

It's taken too much energy already

A dream that resembled a nightmare

A dream that mirrors my present reality

Dreaming and screaming No rest when I am healing

Keeping positive vibes in the day

As my psyche and subconscious torments me at night

Everything I stuff inside

Secrets and insights I keep locked away inside In a box

That's locked in a box

Stuffed in the prison cell I call my min

Attempts to talk to a counselor

But she got furloughed from her job

Pray to talk to God

But the religious ways I've seen perpetrated

The disdain distrust in within my present reality

Hard time moving on from the past when it’s

Embedded in core of my healing

I love the sunshine

Dance in the rain

My sleep however can be so depleting

I’m tired.

So, I sage cry if I must

Swipe the tears that hide my tainted face

Realize that if I died as I lay

I wasn't present for the moment anyway.

Miracle Mile

There comes a time in many of our lives

When all purpose is lost

When there is no one left to call

Alone to your thoughts

Prisoner to heartache and failure

Persistent ruminations of ending it all

Crying in the dark, day dreams don't see fruition

Insecurity restricts you from the choice to even start

Ambition, opportunity and resources are in competition

Constantly conflicting

The weight of the world is overwhelming

Sinking to rock bottom with your back against the wall

Peering over the edge of the cliff of despair

You stumble at the edge

Yet you don't fall

Wiping away your tears

The cliff seems appealing but you don't jump

There's a mustard seed of hope in your heart

Yearning to see the light

Begging for the chance to grow

To blossom into a beautiful lotus

Bearing fruit and flower from the murkiest mud

The reality settles in that mistakes of the past

Have held you captive for far too long

Courage stands up in the presence of fear

And so your faith follows suit because

You have nothing left to lose

Your heart has been bruised

Your scars have yet to heal and

You don't want to die but don't foresee making it through

The reflection in the mirror is

Not the person you wish to see staring back

There is a war between the old and new you

Setting aside ego and pride

Love was a hard lesson

Rejection was protection by God

You lace up your boots

Shake off your tears to stare your demons in the face
And you take a breath and gracefully step away
From the edge of oblivion to the yellow brick road
It is now clear, there is no "Oz" you are the wizard in your life
And a power greater than you is in charge
God/universe/whatever you like, is the director of the show
No need to click your heels because
You now know within the depths of your soul
That you already are and have always been home
We have experienced a time
When defeat seemed to be the only thing in sight
When your income doesn't cover the bills
When your ideas and plans don't suffice
Addiction may have you in its grips
Bound to the shackles of any chosen vice
Depression, paranoia and anxiety
Rule and haunt your life
Relationships are volatile and
pictures don't tell the whole story

Yet you smile for the camera and wait for superficial glory

The blessings is are in the silver lining

And the devil is in the details

Breakdowns are inevitably followed by

A massive breakthrough

There is always a rainbow after the storm

Things change, feelings pass too

If we persevere through trials and tribulations

We won't miss the chance for a miracle.

Honest Appraisal

It seems like everyone has

Their own version of the “truth"

And as some of us evolve

We may cosign and/or redefine

What we have been taught to believe

Then in turn as we grow old trade in what we can no longer use

Convicted to believe what we choose

With or without the evidential proof

God is this and not that...

Recovery is black or white and you're a failure if you relapse

However "keep on coming back"

"Let go of the past"

But accept the rejection you receive because of that

"There is heaven so live by these rules" or

"There is no afterlife so do what you want to do"

If you trust the government

Or follow the sheep like a puppy you're a dummy

One person's trash may be someone else's come up

I heard that from someone

Some of us are convicted and concrete

Some of us indifferent

Maybe ambitious

Educated or ignorant

Could be self-absorbed

Neighborhood playboy or girl next door

Promiscuous, or narcissist

May be completely unattractive or

Highly desired but it doesn't matter at all

You can be the brightest star in the sky

But not everyone will see your twinkle

Not everyone will cheer you on

Unless you have stomped in the same mud someone else does

You will never fully understand

Their struggles, their path

So unless you can lend a hand

Be mindful of your commentary about them

You have no idea what they've been through

Or the power that protects them

Not everyone is meant to be rich, popular or famous

But it seems that's what today's society caters to

The more likes and views the more value in you

The more friends you have to tag in your photos

Makes you more reputable

Toxic positivity is a stroke to the ego

Misguided justice can turn a villain to a hero

And sometimes heroes can be villains too

We all are trudging the same yellow brick road

Yet not all of us have ruby shoes

So we make due and push through

Never giving up although

We so desperately feel like we want to

Seems like "once I get..." and "there"

Is so far away so the present moment

Is taken for granted and fades away

Tomorrow isn't promised today

I once heard someone say

Dying before I have actually lived

And made a difference to my family and friends

Is one of my biggest fears

Somehow the blessings always come at the right time

After the storm there is always a rainbow

And a sun that doesn't need anyone's permission to shine

Growth is painful

Sometimes the miracles are long over due

Sometimes wishes don't come true

We make mistakes, deal with aches and pains

All learning as we go really, all at the same time

Just in different towns, circumstances and situations

We are uniquely the same in different ways.

(Side B) "Pieces of me"

Perfectly Imperfect

And she was perfectly imperfect.

She was flawed yet, beauty graciously caressed her every morning.

Her skin dazzled in the sunlight, sprinkles of cocoa

And heaven complimented her faithfully

Her playful laugh could have

Cured the most debilitating illnesses

She had been admired earlier

Then her parents would have hoped for.

Naivete adorned her like a leather catsuit.

Credulous and far too impressionable

This girl was unfavorably sold many dreams

Her merchants wore many masks

Returning like clockwork to "restock"

Looking at her once pure reflection

This girl grew to detest what she saw glaring back at her

Hell became her safe zone, her hiding place

Trying to fill the emptiness and

Conceal the heartache was her 9-5

Nothing could satisfy her hunger

Her beauty faded and her innocence became careless rage

No matter what she did there was no escaping

The harsh reality of what she had become

And what had been done

Living in fantasy peering over the cliff of death

At the darkest hour her innocence and purity

Lit up the night sky

Coming to a final collapse in desperation

She cried out to the powers divine "Please help me"

For all of her life

Her worth had been estimated by her sexuality

Many times her power of choice

Had been yanked from her

All the love from her mother had been diluted and neglected

Her value system was of course skewed

When this girl fell in love for the first time

It was a love that would revive her and inspire her

She bore a delicate, precious, angelic baby girl

And she finally knew LOVE

Her once failing heart started to beat again

With the motivation of a thousand marathon athletes

She sang, and she danced, she loved, and she prayed

Her world was complete, or so she thought

They returned

The mirror became her enemy once more

And she lost the power bestowed upon her by the divine

Bad decisions led to even worse decisions and

She frequented some of the darkest corners

Years passed and the divine came to visit her again

This time with a vengeance

Whispering in her ear

"Get up"

"Go get your child"

"I love you"

Slowly with many bridges burned along the way

And many hills climbed she found her way

Fighting back her skin began to flicker

A crook nestled in her smile, bridges started to mend

And her once bellowing laugh was heard again

She still gets scared and sometimes questions her existence

But she has grown she has learned and she still loves

Wearing her heart on her sleeve

Has been her best and worst attribute

Still she pressed forward

Holding no grudge she prays for the men

Who wore those masks and

She vows to teach her daughter to learn from her experience

She will never be picture perfect

Her worth is not measured by her physical features

Favors or failure to see peoples true colors

It is by the way that she loves without fear

And her childhood that was betrayed

Girl Left Behind

The girl that got left behind she did not grow up in time

Years passed cities changed though

She was ever still imprisoned by her mind

None to blame

We all bleed the same

Different faces similar pains

She lost her will to fight to be knocked down again

With no hope insight

Tears on the pillow

Desperation fueling her cries

Leaving home to the streets she would roam

Searching bag and bottle for relief

Faithlessly praying for the light

Traumatized by transgression

She owns all guilt and shame

Wears her crown on the ground

Her innocence was never the same

Bursts of anger, violent words

Hurt all who's loved her

A waste of a bill for a phone

No one to connect isolated on her own

Scattered are the fractured pieces of her life she has thrown...

Her only desire is to be someone who belongs
Grow up they say..."Do the right thing"
"She talks so fast she can't hear anything"
A burden to intimacy
Its seems she may be a cause that's long been lost
Its time for her to grow up she is stuck
At a crossroad in her life yet again afraid
Fear has struck; she feels stuck
Hope for stability and better days ahead fizzle
Cast aside through chaos in her head
Beauty once caressed her Love could have been found
Now she grasps for air in a world that shut her out
A power has helped her
Covered by love and grace
The image of her life is a reflection she cannot face
Yearning for change she pleads to find life in a new way
Help from her friends
And a power greater than the people places
And opportunity she's pushed away

Her essence is love though her self-image and esteem is null

She scribbles "void" on her past

And steps into the unknown.

Misinformed

Misinformed, misguided selfish full of pride

Ran from every problem my choices created

Abased and bewildered yet so thankful I am alive

Selfishly searching for a catalyst to attach the error of my wrongs

Too wrapped up in the shell of myself

To feel the cracks of damage in every step

Trails blazed with hell I have left wreckage on

Forgiveness I ask of myself and those I have caused harm

God my source please plug into me so that

I can continue this journey on

Once a fatherless child turned out with lust of men

All to replace the love of him

Currently a child-less mother that mirrored the image

Of my elusive dad

The parent my baby girl doesn't know

The reflection of neglect Judged, hypocritically hated

Forgiveness; empathy

I love you and I want you to know there is no hatred

I understand now that him and I are not unique but afflicted
Relentless Disease

Decisions, choices eluded my wisdom Greed

Self-pity Irrational Fear Manipulation

Outward infringement

Distorted my vision destroyed every relation

Made everyone hate me beauty abandoned

Life was a grave to me

I truly searched like a fiend between the highest of highs

And bottomless lows

Scaled the confines of my self-made prisons

An enemy to my self

A slave to deluded thinking grasping for anything

That could fix my insides

"HOPE"a concept I could no longer envision

Beliefs of my life ending in vain

Consistently pressed against my temple

My Source I call you the God that I know understands

When I am afraid, disposed of and alone

You alone reach and grab my hand

Defeated yet again My foolish “plans”

Poor activity by my own hands

Estranged and alienated- No more family or old friends

Nowhere else to go or run Lost

Am I capable or unwanted is this chance

I have just a "front"

The past taunts and the future is daunt

My cowardice wanted so bad to let life go

You demolished the shovel that threw dirt

On the headstone of my grave

Struggles you turned into to

Purpose

I gotta grow up I must pass through

I call you infinite and divine at times…

You are too magnificent and wide for me to over analyze and define

Angels beside me lighting the paths ahead

Clarity 20/2O please let the demons of the past keep behind me

Fallen stumbled and crawled

Lost turned and confused your illumination and guidance found me

Survived non instigated abuse

She is the gift in the melody of the bird to my left

And the acceptance of failure to do right

Grief and mourning the nest where I can rest

My mothers' condolences

Wrists that carry these hands bled with sickness

And rejection from man

Never have you scoffed at my image or scoffed

At the sight of my hand Thank you, my God

The divinity of nature and boundless coverage

I am coming to understand

You loved me first and always have

Your mercy speaks loud and fierce

With in your grace of one more chance.

Tainted not Jaded

She wasn't jaded she was tainted

Yet her heart still remained

She liked the sunshine

But she learned to dance in the rain and when it hailed

She sprinkled down some salt and prevailed

This is the story of a girl, but it ain't no fairytale

She could never be picture perfect

Compared her insides to other 's outsides

She was always lurking

Never thought she could amount to being anything

Her voice was crippled, and she didn't

Sound the "color coded same"

This little girl used to cut inhaling sobbing breath

Deep slices on her arm she tried to kill herself

People in her family said she wanted some attention

She didn't fit in and at school she always landed in detention

She wasn't the baddest she was average, and she was smart

There was a hole inside her

From the knife in her broken heart
Everyday it felt like she was falling apart
Her first experience with love
Was with three boys at a park
She had a great start to some it seemed
She would smile through her tears
And she would daydream about getting straight A's
And making a change
She dreamed of bright lights and killing it up on stage
But she couldn't control her depression it turned to self-hate
And as the rolled on she had a few dates with rape
Her mom was so distraught her baby girl was wasting away
She did her best to help
But there was nothing left she could say
Her hips got wider; clothes got tighter
And showed off her brown legs
And for the price of her soul
You could take her to bed with you
You would have a time you would never forget

Though in the morning one would always regret

She blazed a trail straight through hell and might never come back

Things got worse she went from this to that

At 18yrs old she went from snorting to smoking crack

At any man's request she'd bend and gently arch her back

Death was in her sights she relentlessly attacked

Through her insanity she bounced through different states

Inhaling smoke clouds and snorting

Off different powdered plates

Anyone could see this little girl had really lost her was

She had been looking for love in all the wrong places

Searching in all the dead ends and all the empty faces.

She would always find that one that wanted to love her

That special guy who would put nothing above her

They loved her smile

Her style and her laugh would make them excited

They'd been with others

But this girl was nothing like them

It always ended pretty badly

For she was extremely damaged

And every one of their hearts

Was left wounded and bandaged

But for her the seed they left

Will be forever planted.

As I Am

The best parts of me are hidden

beneath the illusions of who I feel I "ought to be"

Carefully tucked behind repeated mistakes

That society calls insanity

My trauma responses tell me that

Love can be taken away

As punishment when someone I love is mad at me

Fear and insecurities tell me

Hey will surely reject abandon me

Paranoia dominates the ill motives

I'm certain that anyone I don't know has

And, even if you get close enough to know me

I can't shake the trust issues I have

But I just have to laugh

I am guilty of every single character flaw and

Transgression that the average person has

Divine love carried me through the darkest tunnels

I never thought I'd make it through

Vulnerability is my greatest weakness and strength

Self-sabotage and doubt tends to threaten my livelihood

I am beautiful, no matter what they say

Those who matter don't mind and those that mind don't matter

Anyway I am on a soul journey, slowly finding my way

I am right where I am supposed to be

headed for blessings and brighter days

Gratitude carries me to a joyful state

That no resentment can withstand

Mercy and grace gives me another chance

Learning to love and be loved

To accept myself as I was, as I hope to be as I am.

Frequent Flyer

This world has the potential to negatively affect you

Reject and disrespect you

Make you question the value of your existence

Create your innocence into abuse

Unearthing the predator in you

Sliding down the totem of submission

Becoming the prey, spit out, chewed and used

In such a way that your heart turns cold

Where it was once young and free

It is now bitter and old

Withered roots of disappointment hold space

Where blooming petals of hope and possibility used to grow

The "good old days" long gone

The only ones that survive are "strong"

Hell exists for those who haven't been there already

Heaven is just one floor above

Speaking of, I miss my grandma's hugs

Makes me think of all the people I love

but don't show them enough

And I know, I'm really hard on myself

facing my demons one by one

Collecting the broken pieces of myself

Cultivating my self-esteem

Learning to love who I am, who I was

Appreciating my flaws and my scars

My assets, imperfections, defects and all

Forgiving myself for the things I can't change

Praying for the capacity to handle anything

I don't need fame or notoriety

I just want to be free, joyfully

Constantly I'm challenging my thoughts,

Double-checking my motives...

leading with my heart

Accepting the opportunities I missed

Striving to be a better mom

Healing the past

Focusing on the present

Cherishing experiences with friends and family

I've loved and lost

I can't make sense of life when I look back

Living in such extreme peaks and valleys of hopeless insanity

Reveling in moments of fleeting progress

Surely followed by failure and regress

The lessons I've learned over the years are the real success

So I now live just for today

I do my best not to look back

Only to learn and reflect

Keeping my eyes on the prize so I tilt my chin up

Lace my boots and I look ahead

Trudging forward to my happy destiny

Grateful for everyone and everything I have

Internal Dialogue

I wonder if my heart will ever heal

I wonder if the lies I believe are actually real

I used and ran away from everything

So I wouldn't have to feel

leaving wounds that always have more

layers and depth to reveal

Life has so many joys and blessings

though and I am grateful to receive

The progress I have made so far helps me to have hope

The people in my life that lift me up

Give me courage to believe in me

Sometimes I look in the mirror and don't like what I see

The past seems like yesterday

lacing my present with doubt and insecurities

But I press on eagerly, trusting God and the process

So I can finally be free; a better me

Free from insanity and unmanageability

I look up to the ones that walk a similar journey

Hand in hand with me

Courage is not the absence of fear

But walking forward despite the feeling.

Collecting the Pieces

When I was young I was full of promise

Made honor roll at school Neighborhood friends

Close relationships with my family

Had ever thing I needed or wanted back then

So much personality and light so many activities I was involved in
Life's problems didn't weigh me down

The world was my oyster and I felt like I belonged here

I was very happy at that time My spirit was free

Free to be different

Free to be uniquely me

My confidence was immeasurable

I viewed the world with rose colored eyes

and saw unlimited possibilities

Sadly, freedom didn't last long

Life abruptly wiped the smile on my face

and introduced me to the feeling of

being broken and humiliated

Racism and culture shock caused my spirit to break

Every smile on my face became tears of self-hate

My attitude changed

From that point I never looked at people

Or the world I lived in the same

I didn't fit into a particular box

And I didn't realize it back then

The reason why I didn't fit in

Was because I was meant to stand out

My mom sought after giving me a better education

I am thankful to this day

Even though I was teased all my life for "talking white"

I now know without a doubt

That is some ignorant shit to say

There was a time I was free to be myself

Then the time came when I was not

Rejection and alienation compounded

I was being touched on and groomed

By men twice my age; adult in size

It felt like an unspoken rule

To keep my true feelings and emotions

Tucked deep down inside

I stopped fantasizing and started to realize

Life was nothing like the bliss I had experienced

Once upon a time

The day we moved away everything changed

I felt so out of place

Picked apart by my hair, the way I talked,

my weight, my shape, my race

I became a shell of a girl with no identity

Troubled since then...

I remember when I first picked up a pen

When no one at school would play with me

Ink and paper became my best friend

I did my best to go within

MY first taste of introspection,

I sucked at it moments of relief were never long lasting

I became terrible to deal with

Needless to say, I lost my way

So much insanity

Hyper-sexual

Attention seeking in all the wrong ways

So disconnected from my authentic self

My creator carries me on angels' wings...

My spirit is healing

Transforming through every failure

Glowing up past every shade of hate

Seeking to burden and swarm over me

Rising from ashes of fire

Blazing trails and collecting all the broken pieces of me

Facing my demons

Hitting my knees cleansing my crystals

Engaging and learning from others

Who inspire and believe in me

Thanking God for everything

The melanin in my skin is evidence

Of the goddess energy I inherited

The scars on my body remind me of the warrior within

My boots are laced

Learning something different everyday

My feet blazed a trail in so many places,

Good and bad impressions of me left in many spaces

So many people, so many memories

I'll never forget the love

I'll never forget their faces

On a journey to recapture the little girl I brought into this world

And the innocence I lost

Before the darkness consumed me and

I forgot who I was and what I was made of.

About The Author

Indya Renee began her life in Philadelphia, PA and has traveled from the East to West Coasts residing in California, Texas, Connecticut and surrounding towns but Arizona is her home. Growing up she would have many diverse and influential experiences as she came of age. She is a survivor of sexual misconduct and abuse, racism, mental illness, early onset addiction and many events that crippled her once promising life. Indya however, is someone who chases hope, freedom and healing as well as the desire to help others and bring awareness to these issues. She is an advocate for mental health awareness and is inspired by so many she has seen recover. Personally taking her own recovery one day at a time through many struggles and setbacks, writing and poetry has been a healthy outlet and tool for not only self-expression but introspection. Her writing is raw, uncut, ever growing and developing just as she is. As Indya continues on her journey of self-love, discovery and evolving she invites you to take a peek in to her heart, mind and soul. With various topics covered and a unique touch this is the evolution of her poetic style.

www.ingramcontent.com/pod-product-compliance
Lightning Source LLC
LaVergne TN
LVHW010547160826
845677LV00013B/3033

* 9 7 9 8 8 8 8 6 2 5 3 8 5 *